About This Book

Why is this topic important?

The concept for *Lunch and Learn* is a 55-minute learning session, with a topic selected based on interest and relevance, that addresses the various needs of both employee and employer for learning opportunity and learning support that truly matters. Several trends in training and workplace learning support shorter, smaller, just-in-time sorts of workplace-sponsored training. Off-site, manager-mandated, hotel-hosted workshops and seminars are being cut from corporate budgets everywhere. Organizations are looking for materials that more closely fit with their learning needs: organizational leaders are demanding learning opportunities that are customized for their own employees who are motivated by an immediate need to learn. Organizations are pushing employees to seek the learning they need when they need it, either online or from others in their team or work group. Face-to-face learning situations provide learners an opportunity to awaken awareness, define problems correctly, align resources toward solutions, and collaborate for success.

What can you achieve with this book?

This book focuses on high-interest, high-stress topics that individuals and teams face on a regular basis. Each topic is an attempt to zero in on what employees need and want to talk about and act on, given a new understanding of each topic and its challenges in today's fast-paced working environment. By using this book, organizations can obtain much needed inexpensive, informal, interest-based, self-selected, discussion-enriched on-the-job learning that leads to collaborative action.

How is the book organized?

This book contains 25 *Lunch and Learn* sessions organized into 5 categories: communications, customer service, performance, problem solving, and teams. Each session proceeds according to a similar structure, which begins with a Discussion Starter Handout to stimulate thinking and continues through general discussion and idea generation to problem definition and solution finding. A personal action plan is the goal of each session, and a take-away handout that encourages self-examination and reflection is featured at the end of each session.

About Pfeiffer

Pfeiffer serves the professional development and hands-on resource needs of training and human resource practitioners and gives them products to do their jobs better. We deliver proven ideas and solutions from experts in HR development and HR management, and we offer effective and customizable tools to improve workplace performance. From novice to seasoned professional, Pfeiffer is the source you can trust to make yourself and your organization more successful.

Essential Knowledge Pfeiffer produces insightful, practical, and comprehensive materials on topics that matter the most to training and HR professionals. Our Essential Knowledge resources translate the expertise of seasoned professionals into practical, how-to guidance on critical workplace issues and problems. These resources are supported by case studies, worksheets, and job aids and are frequently supplemented with CD-ROMs, websites, and other means of making the content easier to read, understand, and use.

Essential Tools Pfeiffer's Essential Tools resources save time and expense by offering proven, ready-to-use materials—including exercises, activities, games, instruments, and assessments—for use during a training or team-learning event. These resources are frequently offered in looseleaf or CD-ROM format to facilitate copying and customization of the material.

Pfeiffer also recognizes the remarkable power of new technologies in expanding the reach and effectiveness of training. While e-hype has often created whizbang solutions in search of a problem, we are dedicated to bringing convenience and enhancements to proven training solutions. All our e-tools comply with rigorous functionality standards. The most appropriate technology wrapped around essential content yields the perfect solution for today's on-the-go trainers and human resource professionals.

www.pfeiffer.com

Essential resources for training and HR professionals

Lunch and Learn

CREATIVE AND EASY-TO-USE ACTIVITIES FOR TEAMS AND WORK GROUPS

CAROLYN NILSON

Pfeiffer
A Wiley Imprint
www.pfeiffer.com

Acquiring Editor: *Martin Delahoussaye*
Director of Development: *Kathleen Dolan Davies*
Developmental Editor: *Susan Rachmeler*
Production Editor: *Nina Kreiden*
Editor: *Rebecca Taff*
Manufacturing Supervisor: *Becky Carreño*
Illustrations: *Interactive Composition Corporation*

Printed in the United States of America
Printing   10   9   8   7   6   5   4   3   2   1

This book is dedicated to my family—Noel, Eric, Jeffrey, Kristen, Bob, and Lisa—who remind me every day of the importance and value of talking things through.

Contents

● ●

Introduction: Getting the Most from This Resource 1

COMMUNICATION

1. e-Communication 11

2. Feedback 19

3. Information 27

4. Listening 35

CUSTOMER SERVICE

5. Customer Differentiation 47

6. Customer Expectations 57

7. Customer Satisfaction 65

8. Customer Service Training 73

9. Customer Training 79

PERFORMANCE

10. Change 89

11. Ethics 95

12. Goals 103

13. Priorities 111

14. Recognition and Rewards 119

PROBLEM SOLVING

15. Conflict Management 131

16. Creativity 141

17. Self-Directed Learning 151

18. Time Management 159

19. Valuing Differences 169

TEAMS

20. Alignment 179

21. Building a Team 187

22. Needs of Team Members 195

23. Strategies of Teamwork 203

24. Team Resources 213

25. Team Vision 221

About the Author 229

Introduction

∙∙

Getting the Most from This Resource

● PURPOSE

The purpose of this book is to provide facilitators of learning with a tool for short, structured learning sessions built on reasoned, creative, face-to-face discussion. *Lunch and Learn* reflects today's trends of shrinking training budgets as well as learners' preference for face-to-face learning sessions during the work day. The goals of communication and collaboration in action are primary. Topics in *Lunch and Learn* focus on the key and relevant issues in today's workplaces. *Lunch and Learn* sessions have advantages for employers who need to support employee learning and for employees who need to collaborate, solve problems, and learn from work at work.

● AUDIENCE

The primary audience for this book is a facilitator of learning—this means any person at work with responsibility for teaching another or with a desire to help others learn on the job and contribute directly to the company's bottom line. This might include members of the training or human resources departments, managers, supervisors, team leaders, or team members. The book is appropriate for facilitators in corporations, government agencies, non-profit organizations, schools and colleges, and is a new kind of resource for university programs in adult learning, human resources management, and training.

● BACKGROUND OF THE *LUNCH AND LEARN* APPROACH

Lunch and Learn is structured help for the manager, supervisor, team leader, consultant, or coach in his or her role as instructional designer and trainer. It is a book of learning sessions written using the best principles of discussion and reflection, creative thinking, problem solving, and action planning presented as twenty-five 55-minute learning experiences. The book zeroes in on dozens of high-interest, high-stress topics that need to be talked about in today's workplaces.

It is a book that uses a wide variety of Discussion Starters, or triggers into the topic, that lead to useful *talk* among participants and collaborative or individual action following creative thinking and problem-solving principles. Discussion Starters are meant to challenge and expand participants' ideas, leading to greater depth of understanding and a chance to be heard. Mini-case studies, drawings, stories, maps, symbols, charts, and learning games are some of the kinds of Discussion Starters in these sessions. Topics selected are ones that need to be talked about in a deliberate way at work in order for shared meaning to grow, trust to blossom, communication to flow, and work to progress effectively. Participants are expected to come to a *Lunch and Learn* session based on interest, a need to talk things over, and a desire to learn. The format of the book encourages cross-functional and multi-organizational participation.

● THE STRUCTURE OF THE ACTIVITIES

Each activity in this book is organized the same way and consists of these features:

- *Discussion Starter Handout* (found at the end of each activity) is a strong, creative suggestion meant to stir up participants' thinking at the start of the session. The facilitator should copy each Discussion Starter in sufficient quantity for each participant in the activity to have one as the *Lunch and Learn* session begins.

- *Purpose* briefly describes why this activity is important.

- *Summary* gives the facilitator an overview of main ideas in the activity.

- *Agenda*, including suggested times for each step, lists steps in the facilitation process and assigns suggested time limits for each step.

- *Introduction* includes actions and content that the facilitator needs to do and share with participants early in the session to lead them forward into deeper understanding of the activity.

- *Awareness* typically involves study and discussion of the Discussion Starter Handout, leading into more concrete examples based on information in the Discussion Starter Handout.

- *Examples* encourage participants to apply their awareness of key concepts and issues to workplace examples from their own experiences.

- *Definition* is a feature in which the facilitator guides participants into the beginnings of making change in their own workplace projects.

- *Wrap Up* gives the facilitator suggestions for closing the session.

- *Self-Examination, Reflection, and Action Planning Handout* ties together the challenges represented by the Discussion Starter Handout and discussions during the session. The participant's self-examination and reflection are expected to result in action planning back on the job after the *Lunch and Learn* session is finished.

● SET-UP TASKS FOR THE FACILITATOR

The facilitator is responsible for the following administrative tasks and other aspects of preparation:

- Informing participants of the structure of the program, time and place of meeting, objectives and benefits of the session

- Promoting the *Lunch and Learn* series and this particular session through company media, including e-mail, posters, flyers in mailboxes or the cafeteria, company newsletters, closed circuit TV, websites, and so on; seeking help for promotion tasks from the marketing department

- Handling registration of participants, either in advance of the session or on the day of the session as participants arrive

- Ordering and gathering supplies for each session, including at least one flip chart and markers, extra paper and pencils for participant note-taking, packets of small sticky notes, and handouts in sufficient quantity for all persons registered for the session—plus a few extras for last-minute arrivals

- Being prepared to take charge of each session and lead participants through each activity

- Believing in and advocating the power of learning, both self-directed learning and group learning

- Being able and willing to follow the discipline of the discussion session in order to move participants toward learning goals

- Taking time to preview each session, noting the time estimate for each part

- Being able to expand, contract, or modify each session to involve participants within 1 hour

- Being able to motivate participants to continue with self-examination, reflection, and action planning regarding the topic of the session by using the end-of-session handout back on the job

- Being available after the session to offer follow-up or a listening ear to any participant who needs it as change occurs

- Seeking sponsorship of the *Lunch and Learn* series and of specific sessions from executives, high-level managers, and other workplace leaders

- Providing feedback on participants' learning to executives, managers, supervisors, and team leaders

- Being able to articulate the value of a *Lunch and Learn* session to the organization that sends participants to it, and to guide session selection on the basis of the organization's needs

In addition, facilitators should be guided by some basic techniques while interacting with participants during a session. These specific facilitative techniques can help move discussion forward. They are based on equality of opportunity for all participants, and they are meant to encourage and value diverse contributions. Review them prior to taking on a *Lunch and Learn* session and be ready to implement them. These techniques include the following:

- Create equality of opportunity to speak, not necessarily equal time. Work for individual contributions that best express each participant's style and perspective. Insisting on equal time often defeats the purpose by not recognizing the unique learning characteristics of individual participants.

- Reinforce nonjudgmental listening by encouraging participants to signal understanding and appreciation of another's assumptions and by modeling these behaviors yourself. Encourage use of words like "I think I understand," "Yes, I see your points," "Now I get where you're coming from," and "Tell me more."

- Help participants find common ground as they verbalize their assumptions and points of view; identify common values and opportunities for building relationships. Be specific.

- Correct bias, stereotypes, and cultural distortions within a context of safety for all participants. Use stories, explanations of feelings, and questions about individual needs and wants.

- Seek understanding, not defense of ideas. Probe assumptions; think deep and wide. Ask questions of participants, and encourage them to question each other.

- Don't close the session too soon. If it looks like it will run a lot more than 1 hour, call another session at a mutually agreed time and place to continue from a specific point forward. Closure of the session message and impact can happen the next day or even the next week.

● FACILITATION TIPS

The following set of facilitator tips are specific techniques to help the presentation go smoothly.

Before the Session

- A table should be available to the facilitator on which to place participants' materials and other necessary supplies.

- *Lunch and Learn* sessions are designed around talking, so acoustics are an important consideration: the room should be small enough or the area defined with room dividers so that all participants can easily hear each other speak.

- Review all pages of your chosen *Lunch and Learn* session; look with a presenter's eye. Make notes to yourself in the margins.

- Identify pages you'll use as handouts and copy them in sufficient quantity for all persons registered—plus a few extras. Know when in the session you'll use the handouts to best advantage for your presentation and for their learning.

- A group of twenty persons or fewer is desirable for each session. Check registration numbers and be ready with a date to offer a second session if too many folks have registered.

- Be sure that the *Lunch and Learn* room is equipped with two flip charts, several markers, and masking tape for posting pages on walls if desired. Be sure that extra pads of paper and pencils are within easy reach of participants for note-taking or working through problems. Have at least a dozen pads of sticky notes available for participant use.

- If the organization decides that preregistration is not necessary and that spur-of-the-moment or last-minute commitment is desirable, simply have a session sign-in sheet and pencil on a table near the entry door for attendees to sign their names and contact information (e-mail or phone) in case you need to contact them after the *Lunch and Learn* session. Let them know how to contact you after the session by writing your name and contact information on a flip-chart page and tape it to the wall or a room divider so all can see it.

During the Session

- The Discussion Starter Handout is designed to generate ideas and focus the *Lunch and Learn* session as the session begins. Hand it out to participants as they enter the *Lunch and Learn* room.

- Teach from the Discussion Starter Handout; refer to it throughout the session to reinforce ideas and encourage communication.

- Pick out key words from the text; write them on the flip chart and emphasize them during discussion. Tape flip-chart pages to the wall to help participants remember what was said.

- Ask questions such as:

  Why do you agree?

  Why do you disagree?

  Where and when have you experienced this? Or experienced something similar?

  Why might this be a good idea to introduce here?

  Why might this be a bad idea to introduce here?

- Use examples contributed by participants to encourage further discussion. Experience is a great teacher; leverage participants' experiences to lead the group forward into broader and deeper learning.

- Exchange ideas for solutions; define lessons learned; encourage cooperation with others in the *Lunch and Learn* session; distribute the final handout on Self-Evaluation, Reflection, and Action Planning and challenge participants to action back at work suggested by this handout.

After the Session

- Do a quick e-mail follow-up to the *Lunch and Learn* session about a week after the session. Thank participants for coming and remind them to self-evaluate, reflect, and take action based on what they learned in the session. Encourage participants to engage in self-evaluation or informal evaluation with a buddy from the *Lunch and Learn* session as they put ideas learned in the session to work back on the job. Suggest that these are some techniques to use:

A "Good for Me!" checklist of new ideas or skills to use

Self-recording on the checklist, or recording by an observer

Keeping a frequency count of actions taken to accomplish personal or business goals

Periodic interviews with others affected by your work

Challenging others to higher accomplishment by sharing your progress

Keeping a journal and assessing your growth as time goes by

- Post attendance rosters on the company intranet, newsletters, or by e-mail throughout the company. Motivate others to join future sessions through publicity about the sessions.

Communication

1
·········

e-Communication

···

Is it really better, smarter, faster?

● **PURPOSE**

Getting e-communication right is a challenge in our workplaces. The purpose of this session is to answer the question posed above: "Is it really better, smarter, faster?" by analyzing examples of e-communications, particularly in participants' organizations.

● **SUMMARY**

Forward-looking thinkers and e-learning gurus see the possibilities for a better, faster, smarter workforce; traditional managers and team leaders urge caution. Companies, schools, and organizations of all sorts are both stretching and setting limits on e-mail and other kinds of e-communication in order to find the best approaches.

This activity focuses on the characteristics of e-communication. To begin, participants will review the innovative, trail-blazing presidential campaign of Howard Dean, which used e-communications to build electronically connected, highly focused communities of workers.

Then participants will analyze various kinds of e-communications in their organizations. Effective e-communication practices will be identified and described.

● AGENDA

Step	Time
Discuss the words in the Discussion Starter Handout	15 minutes
Provide examples from the workplace	15 minutes
Describe current and desired practices in the workplace	15 minutes
Wrap up	10 minutes

● INTRODUCTION

1. As participants enter the room, distribute copies of the Discussion Starter Handout and ask them to read it.

2. Begin the session by introducing the topic and why it's important:

   "We're here today to talk about online communication, e-communication. Today's workers in all kinds of organizations use the Internet and the Web to build relationships, teams, and communities. We set up e-meetings; we instant message our colleagues; we e-mail around time zones and across continents. We access, organize, document, and send our thoughts and plans to others in hopes of reducing costs, saving time, and maximizing value. But sometimes we don't truly connect with others and our efforts at communication through cyberspace fail.

   "The handout you received contains words from candidate Howard Dean's presidential campaign, in which his team successfully built a highly focused work community using some of the best ideas in e-communication. Take another look at these words as we begin discussion."

● AWARENESS

3. Allow about 1 minute for participants to take a second look at the Discussion Starter. Point out to them that the three uppermost words are different from the four terms at the bottom of the page. All seven terms represent important concepts in an example of e-communication that worked. Ask participants to try to ignore the politics and concentrate instead on the e-communication ideas and successes of that campaign.

4. Lead a discussion about the basic communication challenges the campaign met by its online techniques. Ask participants whether anyone present had experience with that campaign, and if so, what they considered unique or successful. Ask observers of the campaign what they saw as its e-communication successes. Suggest the following as a start:

- Quantity and intensity of active individual involvement

- Feeding information to people

- Collecting information from people

- Face-to-face spinoffs within a target group

- Timing

- Finding and using expertise

If specifics about the campaign's e-communication results are not mentioned by participants, report to them at least these two statistics: Howard Dean raised more than thirteen times the amount of money online as George W. Bush did during the same campaign period ($40 million from 280,000 online contributors to Bush's $3 million) and had about 25,000 individuals talking to each other on his BLOG for America Web log (Barone, 2004). Note the new names for campaign team members and work processes: Deanlinkers, tabling, flyering. Challenge participants to think about how these concepts and processes could be translated into the workplace.

5. Now change your facilitation focus from campaign specifics to e-communication in general as a transition to examples from this workplace. Consider these typical complaints:

- Technology is mostly a distraction.

- It's about time to return to the tried and true, face-to-face communication methods.

- Computers don't make communication better; they make it worse.

- Instant messaging is not all it's cracked up to be.

- Most employees are using e-mail for gossiping, trading dirty jokes, or complaining.

Urge participants to consider both the positives and the negatives in e-communication as they identify examples from their workplace.

● EXAMPLES

6. Ask learners to describe the ways in which e-communication is happening in their workplace and who benefits or suffers from it. Use two flip charts or two pieces of flip-chart paper posted on a wall next to each other, one for the positives and one for the negatives.

   Label one flip chart "positive examples" and the other "negative examples." Begin with the positives. As the positives are stated by the group, ask the group: "Who benefits?" Then list the negatives, asking: "Who suffers?" List participants' examples yourself or ask one of them to act as scribe. Be specific about who benefits from the positive examples and who suffers from the negative examples. If it's slow getting started with the positives, suggest that the group begin with e-mail. Make two lists, positives and negatives, about e-mail. Then go on to other kinds of e-communication.

● DEFINITION

7. Next, ask the group to come up with a definition of what e-communication should be at this company. Encourage them to use information from the examples on the flip-chart lists. Remind them to acknowledge differences in experiences of the same kind of e-communication and to consider learning styles and personality traits. Think about why the Howard Dean experiment in e-communication worked for his organization. Refer back to the Discussion Starter Handout to encourage discussion. Record ideas on a flip chart to be made into a "definition" statement at the end of the discussion.

8. As discussion of the ideal e-communication for this company proceeds, remind participants of some of the traditional goals of communication: gaining recognition, sharing expertise, breaking down barriers between groups, increasing commitment, building relationships, multiplying team successes, enhancing productivity, and others. Urge participants to think of e-communication as one tool for accomplishing such traditional goals as well as for introducing new ways of doing things. Refer back to the Dean campaign successes.

9. After about 10 minutes of discussion, ask participants to state their definition of what e-communication should be at this company. Record the definition on a flip-chart page for all to see. Revise and edit the definition as participants' ideas are shaped. Aim for a consensus definition.

● WRAP UP

10. Close the session by reviewing the idea that getting e-communication right is a challenge. As they return to their workplaces, suggest that they ask themselves these questions:

    - How are the various tools of e-communication used effectively in work for which I am responsible?

    - Does e-communication here result in a better workforce? If so, how?

    - Does e-communication here result in work getting done faster? In what way?

    - Does e-communication here result in a smarter workforce? To whose advantage? How?

    - How does e-communication here affect the company's bottom line?

    - Should my work use a blended communication approach, that is, traditional communication and e-communication? In what proportion? In what job functions?

11. Distribute a copy of the Self-Examination, Reflection, and Action Planning Handout to each participant and explain that participants can use this as a worksheet to help organize their thoughts.

12. (Optional) Suggest that participants work in teams to develop effective e-communication projects. Allow some time for individuals to seek out others with whom they'd like to collaborate in thinking or design of systems. Encourage them to set dates for collaboration meetings.

REFERENCE

Barone, M. (2004, January 19). The new shoe-leather politics. *U.S. News & World Report*, p. 36.

HANDOUT 1.1
DISCUSSION STARTER HANDOUT FOR
e-Communication

· ·

MoveOn.org

Deanlink.com

Meetup.com

Deanlinkers

flyering

tabling

BLOG
for America

Howard Dean's Presidential Campaign

HANDOUT 1.2

SELF-EXAMINATION, REFLECTION, AND ACTION PLANNING HANDOUT FOR
e-Communication

• •

Self-Examination

Take some time to pledge to yourself to make some kind of change in your use of e-communication at this workplace. Recall and review your own personal successes and failures with e-communication and with communication in general; create a communication journal to document your thoughts.

Reflection

Reflect on the positives and the negatives, defining your own relationship to the persons, groups, and processes written on the flip charts during this session. Examine your own beliefs about the value of e-communication. Ask yourself if you work better, faster, and smarter because of e-communication. Identify specific ways in which you can influence the positive aspects of e-communication.

Action Planning

Resolve to develop a plan for yourself and/or your team to document, assess, and evaluate your current use of e-communication. Establish standards and timelines. Make changes that use e-communication effectively to accomplish your business goals. Write down your top three priorities regarding your own behavioral change to improve e-communication for yourself and the company. Post your priorities in your office.

1.

2.

3.

2
....

Feedback

....

Tell it like it is, buddy

● PURPOSE

Effective feedback processes are important to increase productivity and improve interpersonal relationships in the workplace. The purpose of this session is to describe, explain, and analyze examples of feedback, evaluating them as good or poor.

● SUMMARY

In this activity, participants will review two examples of feedback and discuss which is more effective. Then participants will provide examples of good and poor feedback from their organizations and describe both current and desired feedback practices in their organizations.

● AGENDA

Step	Time
Discuss examples in the Discussion Starter Handout	10 minutes
Provide examples from the workplace	15 minutes
Describe current and desired practices in the workplace	20 minutes
Wrap up	10 minutes

● INTRODUCTION

1. As participants enter the room, distribute copies of the Discussion Starter Handout and ask them to read it.

2. Begin the session by introducing the topic and why it's important:

   "We're here today to talk about feedback. Using feedback effectively is important because it allows us to better communicate with our colleagues, increasing productivity and improving our relationships at work. It's important to remember that the act of providing feedback is a neutral act, neither positive nor negative. It is behavior that is evaluated as good or bad, not the act of giving feedback. This means, of course, that the method you choose for giving feedback requires some forethought so that it can be supportive of your message.

   "The handout you received has two examples of ways to provide feedback—the mother's way and the teacher's way. If you've not done so already, please read the examples now."

● AWARENESS

3. After allowing 1 or 2 minutes for everyone to read the handout, lead a discussion about the two examples, trying to draw out reactions about which one is more effective and why. At this point, don't worry about connecting the examples to the workplace. The examples in the Discussion Starter Handout are meant to encourage participants to expand their thinking. The following questions can be used to help guide this discussion:

- What are some positive aspects of each feedback example?

- What are some negative aspects of each feedback example?

- For each example, what might you do differently to make feedback more effective?

- Do you think one method is preferable to the other? Why is that?

4. After about 10 minutes, bring the discussion to a close and summarize the key elements of effective feedback, including the following points:

- Feedback should be given as close (in time) as possible to the relevant behavior.

- Feedback should be specific, identifying the relevant behavior and any desired changes.

- Feedback should be given in such a way as not to embarrass the recipient in front of others.

- Feedback should be descriptive, not accusatory.

- Feedback should be accepted within the organization as everyone's responsibility.

● EXAMPLES

5. Directing participants to keep in mind the strengths and weaknesses of different feedback methods just discussed, ask them to apply this information to the workplace. Considering such topics as employee performance, customer service, or company-related financial information, ask them to provide some examples of good and poor feedback from their organizations. Make a list of these examples on a flip chart. (You can either list them yourself or ask one of the participants to act as scribe.)

● DEFINITION

6. Next, tell participants that the group will now come up with a "definition" of how feedback is commonly provided within the team or group now as well as how the group would like feedback to be given in the future (if different from current practices).

7. Ask the participants to take a few minutes to think about the amount and timing of feedback, written and unwritten rules about speaking up, rewards and punishments for honesty, how behavior change is encouraged, and so on. Then ask them, as a group, to come up with a definition for feedback as it is currently practiced. You or one of the participants should record the salient points on a flip chart.

For example, if feedback is not widely used or accepted within the team or organization, someone might say, "Currently, people are reluctant to provide feedback because they think others won't be receptive" or "Currently, leaders expect their ideas to be accepted as-is, so feedback is not encouraged." Alternately, if feedback is more commonplace, someone might say, "Currently, the culture in our organization is very supportive of feedback; people are interested to hear what others think."

It's likely that participants will suggest a number of definitions, so some combining and editing will be necessary, which is okay.

8. After you have a current description, ask participants to consider the ideal method for providing feedback and to come up with a future definition for feedback in the organization.

For example, someone might describe the ideal situation as follows: "In the future, people will be open to receiving feedback, and feedback will be presented in a nonjudgmental and respectful manner."

As before, record, combine, and edit the definition as necessary to reflect consensus.

● WRAP-UP

9. To close the session, reiterate the importance of effective feedback, stressing its impact on productivity and positive collegial relationships.

10. Tell participants that although time doesn't permit it in this session, additional self-examination, reflection, and action planning will help them to apply what they've learned in the session to the workplace.

11. Tell participants to think about questions such as:

- Do I give my colleagues enough feedback on important behaviors?

- Do I choose feedback words carefully to avoid misunderstanding?

- Do I sensitively give feedback about bad news as well as good news?

- Do I believe that effective feedback can be the foundation of processes and products of higher quality?

- Am I truly willing to share my accomplishments with others and to rejoice in their good fortunes too?

12. Distribute a copy of the Self-Examination, Reflection, and Action Planning Handout to each participant and explain that participants can use this worksheet to help organize their thoughts.

13. (Optional) Suggest that participants pair up and agree to meet in a week or two to discuss their action plans or suggest some other post-session activity that will help participants carry through on their action plans.

HANDOUT 2.1
DISCUSSION STARTER HANDOUT FOR
Feedback

· ·

"It's, like, really stupid."

Feedback Example Number One

The mother of a high school senior has a calendar taped to the door of the family's refrigerator. On this calendar, she does a daily frequency count of how many times her seventeen-year-old, about to enter the workforce, uses the teen-colloquial word "like" in phrases or sentences.

Feedback Example Number Two

This student's English teacher is also on a campaign against "like" and he makes any student who uses the word as a filler with no meaning write what he or she just said on the blackboard—minus the word "like"—and read aloud to the class the corrected comment some time before the end of the class period that day.

SELF-EXAMINATION, REFLECTION, AND ACTION PLANNING HANDOUT FOR

Feedback

. . . .

Self-Examination and Reflection

Spend some time reflecting on ways in which you give feedback to others. Do you give colleagues enough feedback on important behaviors? Do you choose feedback words carefully to avoid misunderstanding? Do you sensitively give feedback about bad news as well as good news? Do you believe that effective feedback can be the foundation of processes and products of higher quality? Are you truly willing to share your accomplishments with others and to rejoice in their good fortunes too?

Action Planning

Keeping in mind the discussion about "now" and "future" feedback practices at your organization, make a preliminary plan for what you can do to encourage and implement more effective feedback practices. Below, list specific ways in which you can improve communication and personal relationships through feedback.

-
-
-
-
-
-

3

. . . .

Information

. . . .

Now, what was I looking for?

● PURPOSE

Our workplaces are overflowing with information and with challenges regarding
its use. Communication and civility suffer when information is ignored or used
improperly. The purpose of this session is to define and describe useful information
and how it contrasts with information overload.

● SUMMARY

In this activity, participants will discuss the positive as well as the negative aspects
of information and its role in communication. Participants will identify examples
from their workplaces and will suggest ways to make improvements in the use of
information.

● AGENDA

Step	Time
Discuss issues in the Discussion Starter Handout	15 minutes
Provide examples from the workplace	15 minutes
Describe current and desired practices in the workplace	15 minutes
Wrap up	10 minutes

● INTRODUCTION

1. As participants enter the room, distribute copies of the Discussion Starter Handout and ask them to read it.

2. Begin the session by introducing the topic and why it's important:

   "It's easy to get distracted by too much information, especially online. The data in the Discussion Starter come from a typical Google search, in this case, a search on the term U.S. Government Do Not Call Registry. If you haven't already done so, please read the page now. [Allow 2 minutes.] The three elements of the search contain the important information that the searcher was seeking. Data was what the searcher wanted and expected to get. However, the three-page search also contained the following information (acknowledge sneers and chuckles):

   • A flashing banner about restaurant dining

   • Icons for sports, stock quotes, travel, arts and entertainment, and classified ads

   • An announcement about an auto show, in a colorful box within the left margin

   • A four-day weather forecast in many colors near the top of the screen

   • Categorized lists of news, of special reports, and feature stories, listed in the margins

   • An advertisement for 50 percent off home delivery of a local newspaper

   • Four website addresses for telemarketing companies, in colorful boxes in the right margin

"The information presented in this simple search illustrates some of the challenges of information, what to ignore, what to use in response to your motivation for the search in the first place, what to save for later follow-up, what to be legitimately angry over, and so on. We need to approach information in today's workplaces with increased focus."

● AWARENESS

3. After the introduction and references to Google searching, lead a discussion about the elements of the information provided in this particular search. Try to get the group to focus on the intent of the search topic, that is, information about the U.S. Government Do Not Call Registry. Ask participants to comment on the relevant and irrelevant information in this particular search. Refer to the Discussion Starter Handout. Help them to see that it's easy to become distracted by today's online information overload. Use the following questions to help guide discussion:

   • Why do you think online information is especially vulnerable to overload and diminished communication?

   • Do you appreciate the marketing in the margins that's associated with the basic topic of the search? Why or why not?

   • How would you process the marginal information? What steps would you take?

   • What emotions do you have when you receive information like this?

   • What are the ways in which these emotions help or hinder your understanding of the basic topic of the search?

4. After about 15 minutes, bring the discussion to a close and summarize the key elements of information, including the following points:

   • Today's abundance of information can become both a positive and a negative factor in communication.

   • In a search for answers, peripheral information must be identified and set aside for possible later use.

   • In a search for meaning, information either suffers or is enhanced by emotion surrounding it.

- Online information is especially vulnerable to factors that interfere with communication. Poor quality of information, time wasted on irrelevant information, too much information, lack of consistency in focus, irrelevance, and unclear communication channels are some of these factors.

● EXAMPLES

5. Now turn the discussion to examples from their own experiences. Challenge the group to think about the many kinds of communication in this company: face-to-face one-to-one, face-to-face leader-to-group, online one-to-one, online networked, written memos, corporate videos, CDs, DVDs, telephone calls, newsletters, newspapers, team meetings, collaborative efforts across departments or functions or continents, coaching, mentoring, informal learning together, and so on.

   Focus on the problem areas in the various kinds of communication you've just identified. For example, a problem with face-to-face communication is withholding information so you don't hurt somebody's feelings; a problem with telephone calls is rambling and lack of focus; a problem with email is overload; a problem with coaching is not understanding the whole problem. Choose three kinds of communication and ask them to identify the information issue, the problem, and the solutions they've experienced in any of these areas. Use a flip chart to record the positive tips and solutions; title the flip-chart page(s) "SOLUTIONS" and record only the solutions offered during discussion of the examples. (Work the flip chart yourself or ask one of the participants to act as scribe.) Allow about 15 minutes for this activity.

● DEFINITION

6. Next, lead the group into a definition of "information at this company [team/organization]." Try to get a broad definition that suggests various components. Make the definition broad so that later you can relate the examples previously discussed and the solutions on the flip chart to this definition. Read the list of "solutions" on the flip chart to set the group's thinking on the positives as well as the negatives.

7. Begin the definition with the words, "Information here is. . . ." Get consensus on the composite definition.

8. Record this definition on another flip-chart page and post it on a wall where everyone can see it.

● WRAP-UP

9. To close the session, remind participants that communication issues are consistently among the top concerns of workers everywhere. Suggest that the changing nature of information presents major challenges to individuals, teams, and organizations in today's workforce.

10. Challenge participants to leave this session vowing to engage in self-examination and reflection about their own communication problems. Challenge them to return to their workplaces and take action to get and use information more effectively.

11. Tell participants to think about questions such as:

   • Do I use the best process to seek information?

   • Do I carefully define what it is that I expect from information?

   • Have I developed my own system of categorizing information for later use?

   • Can I tell when the information that I find is not the information that I need?

   • Have I first defined my communication need?

   • Do I know good information when I see it?

   • Am I focused on the use of information for communication?

12. Distribute a copy of the Self-Examination, Reflection, and Action Planning Handout to each participant and explain that they can use this handout as a worksheet to help organize their thoughts. Ask them to read it before departing from this session in case they want to refer one more time to the completed flip-chart pages for ideas. Be sure that the pages stating "solutions" and "information at this company" are clearly visible.

13. (Optional) Encourage participants to work in small groups of two or three persons with similar interests in communication and the effective use of information, agreeing to meet regularly to talk over their action plans and help each other take action for improvements that go beyond individual interests.

HANDOUT 3.1
DISCUSSION STARTER HANDOUT FOR
Information

• •

**Information from a Google Search on
the U.S. Government's Do Not Call Registry**

***

A federal appeals court in Denver in February 2004 upheld the U.S. Government's Do Not Call Registry as a valid commercial speech regulation. The 10th Circuit Court of Appeals said that the Registry advances the government's important interests in safeguarding personal privacy and that the First Amendment to the Constitution does not prevent the government from giving consumers this option.

***

The Registry contains approximately 60 million phone numbers of persons who do not wish to be called by telemarketers. Companies that call numbers on the Registry list face fines of up to $11,000 for each violation.

***

Consumers can register their numbers or file complaints online at www.donotcall.gov or by calling 1-888/382-1222. You can also fax a complaint to the Federal Communications Commission (FCC) by faxing the number 202/418-0232.

***

PLUS: flashing banners, stock quotes, auto show, weather, ads

HANDOUT 3.2

SELF-EXAMINATION, REFLECTION, AND ACTION PLANNING HANDOUT FOR
Information

....

Self-Examination

Be somewhat introspective, defining what kinds of things you yourself do best in order to seek, find, and use information to improve communication for yourself as well as for others. Ask yourself key questions: Do you use the most appropriate processes to seek information? Do you carefully define your expectations regarding the information you seek? Do you have a system for categorizing extra information that you find in order to use it later? Do you know what the optimum requirements are for each communication in which you engage? Do you focus on use of information, not just collection of it?

Reflection

Refer back to the items on the flip-chart pages stating "solutions" to information problems and the page defining "information at this company [team/organization]." Reflect on the words and phrases that appeal to you in your own situation. Reflect on what others in the session have said: recognize, value, and build on the positive thoughts of others in the *Lunch and Learn* session.

Action Planning

In your future actions, use a journal, checklist, timeline, or other planning aid to document what you will do in the future to make better use of information.

4
· · · · · · · · ·

Listening

· ·

Listening's a lot more than hearing

● PURPOSE

Effective listening is a foundation for productive relationships with fellow workers, bosses, customers, suppliers, and the community. But a listening experience of high quality involves much more than hearing. The purpose of this session is to explore some simple and some complex issues in listening and begin to build the necessary new skills for effective listening in today's workplace.

● SUMMARY

We know about the standard desirable skills for effective listening: maintaining eye contact while another is talking, being attentive to the message, finding a common space in which to explore common issues, and so on. But listening in today's workplaces involves other deeper or more subtle issues that affect the quality of listening. The kind of listening that's required of today's hassled, overworked, overstressed employees needs to involve the more complicated and less obvious side of the skill in addition to the standard skills we already know. In this session, participants will explore both kinds of issues in listening—the simple and the complex—and resolve to create more effective workplace communication as a result of this exploration.

● AGENDA

Step	Time
Discuss the statistics in the Discussion Starter Handout	15 minutes
Provide examples from the workplace	15 minutes
Describe current and desired practices in the workplace	15 minutes
Wrap up	10 minutes

● INTRODUCTION

1. As participants enter the room, distribute copies of the Discussion Starter Handout and ask them to read it, focusing on the environmental issues that affect listening.

2. Begin the session by introducing the topic and why it's important:

"We're here today to talk about listening. Attentive, careful, respectful listening is critical to effective communication within the walls of the workplace and beyond to customers, suppliers, and the larger community. But our increasingly more diverse workforce and hurried lifestyle works against developing the kinds of listening skills that our demanding workplace requires. We need to explore some of the more complex and relevant issues involved in effective listening and dig deeper into skill requirements beyond the basics. In today's workplace, we need to develop listening skills that overcome disadvantage and diversity, that hear quality through poorly spoken English, and that can compensate for cultural differences. A listening experience of high quality involves much more than hearing the words. The demands of faster, smarter, more diverse workplaces are pushing all our communication skills.

"The handout you've received contains data from an advertisement. It suggests some of the more subtle issues that we need to pay attention to and understand in order to advance our listening skills beyond the fundamentals. If you've not already done so, please read the handout now, paying attention to the statistics and their context."

● AWARENESS

3. After allowing a few minutes for the information in the Discussion Starter Handout to sink in, ask a general question to the group, "So what do you think?"

   Listen to participants' comments for 1 minute or so; then ask them to focus on the environment or life situation of poor children and of affluent children. Ask the group to imagine those four-year-olds listening to their parents talk. Lead a discussion that involves issues of opportunity, structure, and quality—all issues suggested by the information in the advertisement. Guide their thinking with these questions:

   • What do you think of the data that say poor children are disadvantaged when it comes to listening to spoken language?

   • What do you think of the data that say the structural quality of language that children hear is highly related to income?

   • Can you see in these data some more complex listening issues such as access to listening, usefulness of what is heard, and the relationship of quantity of listening to quality of expression?

● EXAMPLES

4. Now shift the focus of discussion to listening issues in this workplace. Write on the flip chart the words to guide discussion about some of these more subtle issues in listening in their jobs and communication encounters with others at work:

   opportunity, structure, quantity, quality

   Suggest that participants think about the advantages various kinds of workers have in the kinds of things they listen to on the job. Ask them to describe examples of listening issues in their work. Keep them focused on some of the more subtle characteristics of deeper issues that go beyond the "maintain eye contact" kind of basics. Write these on a flip chart or ask a participant to act as scribe. Suggest that they think about the factors that affect listening in today's workplaces, and in this workplace especially. Some of these factors could be:

- Time

- Level/position

- Education

- Information

- Expectations

- Knowledge of the company

- Usefulness of the result of good listening

● DEFINITION

5. Next, ask participants to define what characteristics of listening they'd like to see at this company. Help the group to stay focused on description. If complaints begin to surface, bring the discussion back to descriptive characteristics: description is a positive cognitive exercise; complaining is an emotion-filled negative expression. Keep the discussion positive and descriptive. Write the group's definition on a flip chart. Talk through characteristics of listening on the job, working toward a definition that is comprehensive and appropriate for this company. The focus should be a description of the way things should be regarding listening at this company. Remember to acknowledge the contributions and point of view of many participants in the group.

6. Now continue discussion of listening at this company by using the term "listening skills," turning participants' attention to what they might have to do in order to develop the skills they need. Refer to the flip chart(s) to guide their thinking. Ask questions such as:

- In your experience, does listening have "opportunity" dimensions to it?

- How would you, specifically in your job, improve access to information for the benefit of the listener? (Make it more personal? Repeat it more often? etc.)

- Are there structural changes that you personally can make in the nature of information to improve listening for other workers here? (Organize it differently? etc.)

- Can you define several ways to gain some of these more complex listening skills in order to communicate more effectively? (Work to improve access opportunities? etc.)

Encourage participants to use words such as "I think," "I believe," "I value," and "I hear you." Encourage them to pause and reflect on their own relationship to the examples previously provided. Encourage seekers of new points of view. Think of this as an experience of sharing ideas, giving and getting—and listening in new ways.

● WRAP UP

7. To close the session, reiterate the importance of deeper thinking about listening skills in response to today's workplace challenges.

8. Tell participants that additional self-examination, reflection, and action planning will help them to apply what they've learned in today's session.

9. Tell them to think about what they can do to improve their own listening skills and how they can help others in this workplace to improve their listening skills too.

10. Distribute a copy of the Self-Examination, Reflection, and Action Planning Handout to each participant and explain that participants can use this worksheet to help organize their thoughts back on the job.

HANDOUT 4.1

DISCUSSION STARTER HANDOUT FOR
Listening*

••

- By age 4, poor children are exposed to about thirteen million (13,000,000) words used by their parents, mostly in simple sentences.

- By age 4, affluent children are exposed to about forty-five million (45,000,000) words, used by their parents, often in more complex sentences.

*Source: Data from Hoover Institution advertisement for education, *Next: A Journal of Opinion and Research*. Herbert J. Walberg, Distinguished Visiting Fellow, Hoover Institution, Stanford University, Stanford, California.

SELF-EXAMINATION, REFLECTION, AND ACTION PLANNING HANDOUT FOR

Listening

· ·

Self-Examination

If you were a nursery school teacher, what would you do to maximize the communication outcomes of the listening experiences of the 4-year-olds in the Discussion Starter Handout? Think about how listening can be made more effective, considering any or all of the issues discussed in the *Lunch and Learn* session.

Reflection

Reflect on the environment for communication at this company, especially with the situation of folks you personally deal with in your job. Reflect on strategies and actions you personally can take in order to improve the quality of listening within the network of your contacts and colleagues. Ask yourself these questions:

- Do I do any follow-up to conversations to see whether intentions were accurately communicated?

- Can I see the results of speaking and listening that I had in mind?

- Can I see where opportunity, structure, quantity, and quality are related to improved listening?

Action Planning

Take steps to plan your strategies and actions to make your own listening of higher quality. Zero in on specific places and people for influence and change. Begin planning small; make notes to yourself. Give yourself milestones and deadline dates. Make step-by-step plans for more informed thinking, more positive feeling, and more effective action to hone your listening skills and improve communication.

Use this documentation form to begin your action planning. A filled-in example is shown on the facing page.

Strategy:

Action:

Places:

People:

Dates:

Example

Strategy: Learn more about quality standards to improve my understanding of what I hear.

Action: Take the e-learning course offered by the company; follow that with attendance at the American Society for Quality (ASQ) seminar or the four-session quality standards course at the community college.

Places: My own office; the Marriott Hotel; Northwestern Community College

People: Verify the usefulness and quality of these with the company VP of quality.

Dates: Make this a priority for first semester of next year.

_____

_____

_____

_____

_____

_____

_____

_____

_____

Customer Service

5

. . . .

Customer Differentiation

. . . .

One from Column A and one from Column B . . .

● PURPOSE

Customer differentiation is a very important foundation for customer service. It is worth exploring as organizations of all sorts compete for customers and for their loyalty. The purpose of this session is to introduce participants to various kinds of customer differentiation and to analyze the standards and practices of their organizations.

● SUMMARY

One way to define employees' customers is "the people who use the products of their personal work" (www.baldrige.nist.gov/Progress_Leaders.htm). But "people" is an all-encompassing term, not particularly helpful in the kind of market research that distinguishes one kind of customer from another. In this session, participants will examine several approaches to customer differentiation. They will also discuss how their organization differentiates customers.

● AGENDA

Step	Time
Discuss the example in the Discussion Starter Handout	5 minutes
Analyze several examples of customer differentiation	20 minutes
Describe current and desired practices in this company	20 minutes
Wrap up	10 minutes

● PREPARATION

Prior to the session, create a flip chart that shows the scale and five items listed in Step 9 (NIST, 2004, p. 3).

● INTRODUCTION

1. As participants enter the room, distribute copies of the Discussion Starter Handout and ask them to read it.

2. Begin the session by introducing the topic and why it's important:

   "We're here today to talk about customer differentiation. This is the term given to the strategies your company uses to identify and differentiate the people who use the products of your work. But 'people' is an all-encompassing term, not particularly helpful in the kind of market research that distinguishes one kind of customer from another in order to serve them better. Customer differentiation is a very important foundation for customer service and is worth exploring as organizations of all sorts compete for customers and for their loyalty.

   "The handout you received reports the experience of one customer who doesn't want to be differentiated! If you haven't read the handout yet, please do so now."

● AWARENESS

3. After allowing about 1 minute for everyone to read the handout, lead a discussion about the "customer" in the handout. The following questions can be used to help guide discussion:

- What information does the unnamed company use to differentiate customers?

- Who in this room has had a similar experience to that of this customer, who is angry and frustrated and doesn't want to be treated as a number on some list?

- Can you think of better ways for marketers to accumulate information about customers and potential customers and to differentiate one from the other?

● EXAMPLES

4. Tell the group that you have three examples of customer differentiation that you'd like them to listen to, paying attention to the different strategies represented. Suggest that they make brief notes to themselves in the white space on the Discussion Starter Handout.

Example A: Publishing

In religious publishing there is a book phenomenon, *The Purpose Driven Life* by Rick Warren (2002), a *New York Times* advice best-seller for approximately seventy weeks with fifteen million copies sold in its first two years of publication. How this book is marketed tells something about the particular way its customers are differentiated. These are some of the techniques used to build and differentiate the customer base: campaigns within churches called "40 Days of Purpose"; selling resource kits to church pastors that include sermons, a teaching video, and posters; offering copies of the book to members of church congregations at half-price; a pastors' website that sends out a weekly email "toolbox" of ideas to over 100,000 subscribers; instructions on how to map a geographical area in order to bring in unchurched people; motivating readers to purchase ancillary related products like music CDs and other purpose-driven books. This is a case in which various products are targeted to "differentiated" customers within the total customer base.

Example B: Health Care

In contrast, here's an example from the field of health care, focusing on customer access and the processes of communication and feedback. An applicant for the Baldrige National Quality Award in Health Care is asked, "How do you determine key contact requirements for each mode of patient and other customer access?" and "How do you ensure that these contact requirements are deployed to all people and processes involved?" The wording in these questions hints at the importance of customer differentiation. In the Relationship Building section of the Baldrige Health Care award guidelines, the criteria include patient/customer access to seek information, obtain services, and make complaints.

Example C: Retail Sales

An applicant for a job at the local store in a retail chain was interviewed for a sales position. She was asked what she believed was the main job of a salesperson. The applicant quickly responded that the main job was to focus on that individual customer and make that customer happy, by talking about the new looks for the season, by showing the customer the sale items, and by finding accessories and related items to complete the total outfit look. This job applicant got it right—recognizing that customer service often means seeing a single customer as differentiated in terms of all of the fashion advice and products carried by the retailer. Not only the broad customer base but also the individual customer deserves to be served appropriately and with particular kinds of enthusiasm.

5. As participants are thinking about the three examples they've just heard, write these words on the flip chart to guide discussion of the examples:

   - Add-on products

   - Patient/customer access to information

   - Patient/customer feedback processes

   - Seeing the customer as an individual with many needs

6. Lead a discussion that compares and contrasts the add-on products of the publishing company with the add-ons in the retail sales operation. Ask

the group to comment on the first and last bulleted items above and these two kinds of businesses they represent. Ask the questions:

- What are the differences between the publishing company's approach and the retail salesperson's approach?

- Have you ever been one of those kinds of differentiated customers, and how did you feel about it?

7. Then focus on the two health care bullet items and lead a discussion about information and communication issues regarding patient (customer) differentiation in health care. Ask the group:

- Are you aware of being a member of a differentiated group regarding health care access?

- What are the communication and feedback processes put in place by your health care providers to serve you as a customer?

- Do you appreciate being differentiated?

● DEFINITION

8. Now turn participants' attention to their organization's customers for a definition of customer differentiation here. Lead a discussion based on the following questions and record answers on the flip chart, or ask for a volunteer scribe to record answers:

- How does this company find customers?

- How does this company differentiate them one from the other?

- Do you use "leading indicator groups" of key customers to inform your creative processes? Sales?

- Can you spot customer trend leaders? Do you pay attention to them in ways that are different from your typical customer relations?

- Do you focus on creating knowledge, not just on accumulating or managing it?

- What role(s) can you imagine for customers, especially differentiated customers, in fostering innovation? In expanding your customer base?

- Can you describe your customers, those who use products of your personal work?

9. In a final activity of definition and focus on this company's leadership and its customers, tell participants that this will be a "show of hands" rating exercise. To introduce it, read the following paragraph:

> "The Baldrige Quality Award program publishes through the National Institute of Standards and Technology (NIST) a self-administered three-page questionnaire for 'leaders.' It is available free of charge and downloadable from the Baldrige website, www.baldrige.nist.gov/ Progress_Leaders.htm. Questionnaire items are self-rated according to a 5-point scale from strongly disagree (1) to strongly agree (5). I'm going to read the five statements from the customer and market focus section."

Show the previously prepared flip-chart page and explain the rating scale to participants. Ask them to vote by show of hands according to their experience with customers here. Record participants' opinions on the flip chart under the appropriate number; for example, if eight participants disagree with item 1, record "8" under number 2 on the rating scale.

1, strongly disagree; 2, disagree; 3, neither agree nor disagree;
4, agree; 5, strongly agree

$-$ 1   2   3   4   5 $+$

1. Our employees know who their most important customers are.

2. Our employees keep in touch with their customers.

3. Their customers tell our employees what they need and want.

4. Our employees ask if their customers are satisfied or dissatisfied with their work.

5. Our employees are allowed to make decisions to solve problems for their customers.

Information you've gathered from Steps 8 and 9 above should give you a pretty good idea of how customers are differentiated at this company. Ask the group to comment on the results of the "show of hands" rating, and ask whether they like what they see as this company's profile.

● WRAP UP

10. To close the session, reiterate the importance of customer differentiation that goes beyond area codes and zip codes, stressing the values of communication, service, and loyalty.

11. As participants go back to their jobs, suggest that they take the rating scale back with them for referral from time to time. Tell them that it is reproduced on a Self-Examination, Reflection, and Action Planning Handout that you will now distribute to them. Suggest that they copy the group's ratings onto their handouts for future reference.

12. Distribute a copy of the Self-Examination, Reflection, and Action Planning Handout to each participant and explain that participants can use this as a worksheet to help organize their thoughts.

REFERENCES

National Institute of Standards and Technology (NIST). (2004). *Are we making progress as leaders?* Questionnaire. Washington, DC: U.S. Department of Commerce. Available: www.baldrige.nist.gov/Progress_Leaders.htm

Warren, R. (2002). *The purpose driven life*. Grand Rapids, MI: Zondervan.

DISCUSSION STARTER HANDOUT FOR
Customer Differentiation

· ·

I'm a customer already. . . .

I never give out any information about myself, especially my e-mail address and number of kids.

I throw them off by saying I live in the Bahamas.

It's not my job to give them lots of details for the benefit of their marketing organization.

HANDOUT 5.2

SELF-EXAMINATION, REFLECTION, AND ACTION PLANNING HANDOUT FOR
Customer Differentiation

● ●

Self-Examination and Reflection

As you think about serving your customers better to their advantage and to yours, reflect on the "show of hands" rating scale in which you participated at the *Lunch and Learn* session. It is reproduced here* for you to keep in your files. As you think about the five statements, personalize to yourself by substituting the word "I," "My," or "Me," for example, "I know who my most important customers are," "My customers tell me what they need," and "I am allowed to make decisions to solve problems for my customers."

1: strongly disagree   2: disagree   3: neither agree nor disagree
4: agree   5: strongly agree

$-$ 1   2   3   4   5 $+$

1. Our employees know who their most important customers are.

2. Our employees keep in touch with their customers.

3. Their customers tell our employees what they need and want.

4. Our employees ask whether their customers are satisfied or dissatisfied with their work.

5. Our employees are allowed to make decisions to solve problems for their customers.

---

*Source: From "Are We Making Progress as Leaders?" Questionnaire, www.baldrige.nist.gov/Progress_Leaders.htm. National Institute of Standards and Technology, U.S. Department of Commerce, Washington, DC, February 2004, p. 3.

Action Planning

Resolve to meet with others in the *Lunch and Learn* session or others in key positions around the company to begin planning specific actions to take in order to better differentiate your customers and thereby serve them and the company better. Jot down on this worksheet the names of persons you'd like to talk with and the dates by which you'd like to initiate these discussions.

Persons   *Dates*

-

-

-

-

-

-

-

6

· · · · · · · ·

Customer Expectations

· ·

Happy talk and designer uniforms, or comfortable seats and on time?

● PURPOSE

It's important to know what your customers expect of you in order to keep growing your business. The purpose of this activity is to analyze selected products and services to define customer expectations and to translate that analysis to this company's ways of defining and responding to expectations of its customers.

● SUMMARY

Customers have expectations for products that work and honest services. Often, companies and teams don't pay enough attention to what specific customers want, need, and expect, with the effect of limiting business transactions. In this activity, participants will examine issues in customer expectations by analyzing several examples from different businesses: airlines, auto manufacturing, and money-lending. Then, participants will describe ways of defining customer expectations at this company.

● AGENDA

Step	Time
Discuss the example in the Discussion Starter Handout	10 minutes
Analyze varied examples from the workplace	20 minutes
Describe current and desired practices in the workplace	20 minutes
Wrap up	5 minutes

● INTRODUCTION

1. As participants enter the room, distribute copies of the Discussion Starter Handout and ask them to read it.

2. Begin the session by introducing the topic and why it's important:

> "This session today will focus on customer expectations, those ideas customers have about products and services sometimes even before companies create them. We'll talk about how we, as providers, can tap into those expectations early in our business processes to find out what our customers really expect of us. In this activity, we'll examine issues in customer expectations by analyzing several examples from different businesses: airlines, auto manufacturing, and money-lending. Then, we'll turn our attention to this company and describe ways of defining customer expectations here.

> "The handout you received contains information about United Airlines' introduction of its low-cost carrier, Ted. Year 2004, the year Ted was introduced, saw an extraordinary amount of customer expectation talk about the airlines and airline travel. Early year 2005 saw an industry-wide competition on fare price. If you haven't read the handout, please do so now."

● AWARENESS

3. Allow 1 minute or so for participants to read the handout. Ask them to pay attention to the key ideas of customer service in it.

4. Begin a discussion about participants' expectations of airline travel. Ask for a volunteer to write their responses on the flip chart. After you've created a list

---

of at least six items, ask the group to pick out the top three and number them in order, 1, 2, 3.

5. Now ask the group what they *don't* expect from airline travel and in fact consider unnecessary. Record these on another flip chart. Ask the group whether any airline ever asked them what they expected as customers. Conclude the discussion with a comment that all the marketing pizzazz, fun and games on board, cool colors and groovy sounds won't matter if the simple customer expectations for comfort, timing, value, and safety are not defined accurately and met. Ask the group if they think Ted was a good customer expectation strategy for troubled United Airlines in year 2004. Why or why not?

● EXAMPLES

6. Now introduce two other examples, one from auto manufacturing, Nissan Motors of Japan, and one from money-lending, E-Loan from California. Tell the group that these both reflect today's environment of global business opportunity and even greater need for getting customer expectations right. Write on the flip chart the words "knowledge embedded in the market" and "money problems solved by speed." Read aloud the following two examples, Nissan Motors and E-Loan, suggesting that participants listen carefully for evidence of customer expectations.

> "Ikujiro Nonaka and Hirotaka Tageuchi's (1995) classic book, *The Knowledge Creating Company,* contains many stories of creative product development. Among these is the story of Nissan Motors, which set about developing a car that would be designed to ride on the Autobahn in Germany. The authors make a point that in cross-cultural customer creation and product development, it is imperative that cross-cultural socialization take place during the creative process. Experience driving on and riding on the Autobahn and living within German society was essential to accurately defining customer requirements, expectations, and preferences. Nonaka and Tageuchi make the point that 'knowledge is embedded in the market' and that the more mature the market, the more intense and frequent the cross-cultural experience of that market has to be (pp. 231ff). Deep interaction between the development crew and the market was Nissan's initial customer service strategy—even before a product was designed or named. The authors believe that insight, intuition, hunches, emotions, and learning from experience about the

potential customer can only be obtained by immersion in the customer culture. They also believe that knowledge is best spread at the group level, through processes such as discussion, sharing experience, and observation. Nissan's Japanese crew spent as much time as they needed before product design to figure out customer expectations.

"E-Loan, a money-lending company in California, knows that its customer base is often in trouble financially and that speed of processing is a strong customer value and expectation. E-Loan gives its customers a choice of having their loan paperwork processed in India if they want one-day service, or in the United States if they'll settle for two-day or more service. E-Loan reports that more than 80 percent of its customers choose India (Conda & Anderson, 2004). Whatever emotional angst goes along with offshoring to India is overridden by the company's ability to deliver the kind of service customers need and expect. Add to this the fact that the E-Loan customer has a choice—a critical involvement in the solution to his or her financial problem—and the expectation that this company can and will 'work with me.'"

7. Referring to the Nissan example, ask participants whether they know of any global company that has a similar effective customer expectations strategy. Refer to the E-Loan example of customer creation based on successful understanding of who their customers are and what they expect. Ask the group if they know of similar customer expectations for ultra-fast service either in this company or in another company. Introduce the terms "deep customer focus" and "customer advocacy" as concepts in defining customer expectations illustrated by the Nissan and E-Loan examples.

● DEFINITION

8. Ask the group to focus now on their own customers at this company and define what they believe are at least three expectations for customers here. Record their ideas on the flip chart. Gather information; withhold judgment; share concerns. If the group participants come from various organizations, each with different customers, you might need more than one flip-chart page. As participants respond, ask them to first identify their customer, then state the expectations that the customer has for products or services from employees.

9. After you've collected a representative group of participant responses, ask the contributors how they found out what their customers expected. Go down the

list on the flip chart, one by one, to arrive at a definition of what the processes of defining customer expectations at this company currently are.

10. Conclude this definition discussion by asking the group if they'd suggest any modifications to the current approach to defining customer expectations here. Add modification suggestions to the current flip chart using stars or underlined words for emphasis. Validate what currently is, but allow room for other ideas.

● WRAP UP

11. After about 5 minutes of discussion, distribute copies of the Self-Examination, Reflection, and Action Learning Handout to each participant and explain that this can be used as a worksheet to help them remember this session and its lessons.

REFERENCES

Conda, C., & Anderson, S. (2004, March 29). Traders are not traitors. *The Weekly Standard*, pp. 21–23.

Nonaka, I., & Tageuchi, H. (1995). *The knowledge creating company.* New York: Oxford University Press.

DISCUSSION STARTER HANDOUT FOR
Customer Expectations

....

Here's . . .
Ted!

"We are exci-TED
that we have depar-TED,
and we are motiva-TED to serve you."

Co-pilot's announcement on take-off of **Ted,**
United Airlines' low-cost carrier, February 12, 2004
(*The Wall Street Journal,* February 13, 2004, p. W1;14)

HANDOUT 6.2

SELF-EXAMINATION, REFLECTION, AND ACTION PLANNING HANDOUT FOR

Customer Expectations

• •

Self-Examination and Reflection

As you think about your own work and your customers, look inward to define a customer expectation strategy for your work. Recall the customer expectations discussion of the three businesses described in the *Lunch and Learn* session: United Airlines' Ted, Nissan Motors, and E-Loan, three different kinds of businesses. As you read this, think about the important concepts of deep customer focus and customer advocacy. Reflect on the positive changes you could make in your work to meet and even exceed your customers' expectations.

Action Planning

Take some time to identify what you can do differently to create a deeper customer focus and customer advocacy and to explain how these things can be started. Share your ideas with others at this company who are also involved with these same customers. Resolve independently or together to take action and identify critical time points for doing so. Follow this format as you document your ideas.

Customer's name _____

_____

Ideas for deeper customer focus _____

_____

_____

_____

Ideas for customer advocacy _____

_____

_____

_____

_____

_____

Customer's name _____

_____

Ideas for deeper customer focus _____

_____

_____

Ideas for customer advocacy _____

_____

_____

_____

_____

_____

7
. . . .

Customer Satisfaction

. . . .

More than the smiles test

● PURPOSE

Satisfied customers are the foundation of any business. However, we don't always know how to identify the things we do in our daily jobs that lead to customer satisfaction. The purpose of this session is to practice skills of analysis that relate to customer satisfaction.

● SUMMARY

In this activity, participants will learn about ways to analyze customer satisfaction and then apply those analysis skills to this workplace.

● AGENDA

Step	Time
Discuss the Discussion Starter Handout	10 minutes
Learn about customer satisfaction analysis	25 minutes
Describe current and desired practices in the workplace	20 minutes
Wrap up	5 minutes

● INTRODUCTION

1. As participants enter the room, distribute copies of the Discussion Starter Handout and ask participants to read it.

2. Begin the session by introducing the topic of customer satisfaction and why it's important:

   "Satisfied customers are the foundation of any business. However, we don't always know how to identify the things we do in our daily jobs that lead to customer satisfaction. We often don't ask the right questions of our customers and therefore receive feedback that's incomplete. In this activity, you'll learn about ways to analyze customer satisfaction. You will then apply the same kinds of analysis techniques to this company and your customers.

   "The Discussion Starter Handout you received contains the old familiar saying 'You can't tell where you're going if you don't know where you've been.' Take this back to your office and keep it as a reminder to 'know where you've been' regarding the customers you serve and the things you do well or could do better to serve them."

● AWARENESS

3. Referring to the Discussion Starter Handout, ask participants how they think the statement applies to customer satisfaction.

4. If no one mentions it, be sure to bring up the point that it's important to have a record of customer satisfaction measurements so that an organization has some idea of what its strengths and weaknesses are and where to direct attention and resources to improve customer satisfaction.

● EXAMPLES

5. Give the Analytical Handout for Customer Satisfaction to all participants, suggesting that here's a typical approach one of them might use in analyzing customer satisfaction and in learning from feedback. Refer to this handout for ideas as you break into small teams for the next activity.

6. Ask each group to come up with several customer satisfaction measures that the company uses and to provide specific examples of feedback they've received or are aware of on these measures.

7. Reconvene the entire group and ask one member of each group to report out the results of that group's discussion.

● DEFINITION

8. Now ask the group to select the areas of the business that have the most impact on customers of this company. Name a function, such as manufactured products, or Internet services, or the process of selling. Within each function, then identify several potential problem areas for customers. Talk through ideas as a group.

Using the format below, ask for a volunteer to record the group's analysis on the flip chart, aiming for at least three different business functions.

Function A: _____

potential problems: _____

_____

_____

_____

Function B: _____

potential problems: _____

_____

_____

_____

Function C: _____

potential problems: _____

_____

_____

_____

9. To finish this definition part of the activity, ask participants to think of themselves as initiators of a customer satisfaction study here at this company. Lead a discussion about "how." Ask the following questions:

- How do you ensure that what you measure can be acted on?

- How do you determine customer satisfaction and dissatisfaction?

- How do these determination methods differ among customer groups?

- How do you use customer feedback information to make improvements?

- How do you effectively involve current customers in ways to attract new customers?

● WRAP UP

10. To close the session, reiterate the importance of careful analysis of business operations in order to increase the probability of customer satisfaction in the jobs we do.

11. Explain to the group that additional self-examination, reflection, and action planning back on the job regarding the satisfaction of their customers is an important follow-on to this *Lunch and Learn* session.

12. Tell participants to be thinking about these kinds of questions:

- Can I actually act on the measurements I use?

- Do I know who else besides me is involved with my customers?

- Can I identify other processes or transactions that affect my customer interactions?

- Do I have authority to do what it takes to improve customer satisfaction?

13. Distribute a copy of the Self-Examination, Reflection, and Action Planning Handout to each participant and explain that participants can use this worksheet to organize their thoughts.

DISCUSSION STARTER HANDOUT FOR
Customer Satisfaction

· ·

You can't tell

where you're going

if you don't know

where you've been.

Old adage

HANDOUT 7.2
ANALYTICAL HANDOUT FOR
Customer Satisfaction

. . . .

The four steps below are ways to analyze customer satisfaction feedback. For this handout, examples from a manufacturing company are used, but the techniques can be applied to all types of businesses and organizations.

Step 1: Identify the most important problems reported by customers, for example: problems in delivery time, installation glitches, shipping errors, product quality defects, and so on. A simple checklist or frequency count over a specified period of time is a good start.

Step 2: Turn these numbers into a bar graph or pie chart in order to see relationships. Calculate the percentage of complaints in each problem area.

Step 3: Now analyze the data in a different way, for example, the cost to fix these problem areas: delivery time, installation glitches, shipping errors, product quality defects, and so on. You might find, for example, that while shipping had the highest percentage of problems, the problems in quality would be the most costly to fix because new equipment or new hires might be indicated.

Step 4: Then look more deeply into the problem areas identified by customers as the greatest problems: If it's quality, look further into exactly what feature of the product is bad quality, for example, the paint finish, the ball bearings, the welding, the wiring, and so on. Keep getting deeper and deeper into the details of problems identified, and learn as much as possible from customer feedback. Increase and multiply awareness by more than a "smiles test" regarding customer satisfaction.

Lunch and Learn

SELF-EXAMINATION, REFLECTION, AND ACTION PLANNING HANDOUT FOR
Customer Satisfaction

· ·

Self-Examination

Return to the message on the Discussion Starter: "You can't tell where you're going if you don't know where you've been." Post this in a prominent place in your office or workstation as a reminder to find out "where you've been" in terms of serving customers.

Reflection

Also reflect back on the various discussions in the *Lunch and Learn* session. Zero in on places where you can contribute expertise or interest in measurement, setting standards, gathering customer feedback, communicating with others you don't usually communicate with, provide leverage, provide sponsorship, and so on.

Action Planning

Choose at least one function in which you can take action immediately to improve customer satisfaction, and seek, receive, and act on feedback. Resolve to begin an action plan within the next week.

8

....

Customer Service Training

....

"This isn't a technical question...."

● PURPOSE

Customer service in recent years has taken on new meaning as knowledge work and its customers have spread worldwide. Service providers reside in many countries, serving customers far away as well as close to home. The purpose of this session is to examine the new look of customer service and to suggest tips for training customer service workers.

● SUMMARY

The Internet and other high-speed communications advances have made it attractive to companies to offshore communication-dependent, knowledge work to locations around the world. Work done offshore often contributes substantially to a company's profit and is likely to remain a favored business practice for many years. In this activity, participants will read and discuss an actual experience of providing customer service and identify some training needs that are apparent in this experience.

● AGENDA

Step	Time
Discuss the Discussion Starter Handout	15 minutes
Analyze personal story from a training perspective	20 minutes
Describe current and desired practices in the workplace	15 minutes
Wrap up	5 minutes

● INTRODUCTION

1. As participants enter the room, distribute copies of the Discussion Starter Handout and ask them to review it, or ask for a volunteer from the group to read it as if he or she were telling a story. Allow several minutes for this.

2. Begin the session by introducing the topic and why it's important:

   "If you've read any business publications over the last year, you no doubt have seen information and opinions about trends in customer service, including sending work to other countries. Politicians and academics, TV pundits, authors, journalists, and executives are all involved in reporting the news and sounding forth their comments. You also, no doubt, have some facts and opinions of your own about offshoring in general and offshoring customer service in particular. In fact, you probably have been a customer served through an offshore office. Maybe you've been driven to express a longing for the old days when life was simpler. Maybe you've even thought about what kind of training that customer caller had.

   "We know that for many reasons offshoring customer service is not universally well-received by its intended customers. Training might be a contributing factor to its success or its failure. In this session we'll examine the Discussion Starter Handout, A True Story of Customer Service, and build a set of tips for customer trainers. Take another look at the handout before we begin analyzing it."

● AWARENESS

3. Ask for a volunteer to work at the flip chart as you facilitate the discussion of challenges to today's customer service operations, wherever they are located.

4. Turn the group's attention to the handout, and ask them to find the teachable moments in the narrative, that is, the places where better or different training could have helped the caller as well as the customer. Ask the volunteer scribe to list these.

   Examples are how to transfer calls to other departments, which products are in which department, the product provider's lines of responsibility, call center etiquette, correspondence between catalog entries and computers residing in customers' offices.

5. If the group has a hard time getting started, suggest one or more of the examples.

● EXAMPLES

6. Ask participants whether they've ever been in a similar situation and ask them to describe their experiences. Ask them to identify moments in those transactions in which better or different training could have helped. Remind participants to be respectful of others' points of view and experiences and to offer useful feedback to those with whom they might disagree. Seek understanding.

7. Return to the Discussion Starter Handout and focus on the municipal computer consultant's experience. Ask the group these questions:

   • What business questions does this transaction raise?

   • Was this the most efficient way to do business?

   • Was this good customer service?

   • Did repeating a simple story about a purchase of a printer six times over the course of 90 minutes make this a customer who is likely to recommend shopping from this catalog to his other municipal clients?

- Who absorbs the cost of the consultant's time on the phone? Tax dollars? A major issue is that, while very capable of understanding the language and being able to speak nicely on the phone, the call center staffers did not quite understand the nature of the business transaction that was trying to be made, and in fact contributed to the customer's great dissatisfaction, inefficient transaction, and waste of time.

8. Finish discussion of the personal story by considering these questions:

   - What kind of training do you think the customer service representatives had?

   - What kind of training should have happened?

   - Whatever happened to the business goal of efficient operations?

● DEFINITION

9. Now ask the group to define this company's customer service practices and customer service training needs. Use a flip chart to record the training needs.

● WRAP UP

10. Tell participants that, as they return to their jobs, they should do some deeper introspection about how they can affect their organization's success through the right kind of customer service training.

11. Distribute a copy of the Self-Examination, Reflection, and Action Planning Handout to each participant and explain that participants can use this worksheet to help organize their thoughts.

DISCUSSION STARTER HANDOUT FOR
Customer Service Training

. . . .

A True Story of Customer Service

In my town, a computer consultant ordered a printer for the town treasurer out of a catalog. Once the printer was installed, the consultant discovered that the new printer was incompatible with the operating system on the treasurer's computer, although the catalog made no mention of this. The uninformed or misinformed consumer had to return the printer and exchange it for one that did work with the town's computer.

I happened to be sitting in the office in which the consultant made the phone call to the customer service number, at which time, after listening to the whole story, the person on the receiving end of the phone call transferred the customer to Tech Support. Tech Support listened to the whole story and said, "This isn't a technical question," to which the customer responded that he certainly concurred—it was a marketing question. Tech Support then transferred the customer to another call center staffer, who listened to the whole story, said he'd have to transfer the customer to yet another person—and another—and another—and another, a total of five more transfers. Each time the whole customer story was repeated, until finally, at the end of 90 minutes on the phone, someone named Paul understood the problem, agreed to absorb the shipping costs to return the useless printer, and apologized for the aggravation. Each person receiving the customer's call spoke with an Indian accent, was very polite, and efficiently transferred the call when he or she couldn't handle the problem.

HANDOUT 8.2

SELF-EXAMINATION, REFLECTION, AND ACTION PLANNING HANDOUT FOR
Customer Service Training

••

Self-Examination and Reflection

Examine your own feelings about customer service today. The practice of off-shoring customer service knowledge work is destined to be around for some time as politicians, legislators, and business lobby groups continue to think in terms of "geopolitics." As you continue to reflect, focus especially on customer service experiences you've had, and identify customer service training strategies appropriate to the new global customer service workforce.

Action Planning

Resolve to understand the learning needs of today's new knowledge workers. Read and talk with people who are doing customer service work in low-level call centers and in high-level software creation or medical report interpretation. Solidify your grasp of the many issues involved. Think about the many kinds of customer service and the business forces that drive customer support offshore. Take action to sponsor, design, or deliver customer service training to customer service personnel with whom you interact.

9
....

Customer Training

....

Talk business, not education

● PURPOSE

Customer training is a strategy for business success, and one that is sometimes
overlooked. The purpose of this session is to develop a sensitivity to business
opportunities through the training of customers.

● SUMMARY

Customer training is different from customer service training, which tends to focus
on the soft skills of interaction. Customer training involves teaching customers the
hard skills they need to make products work as advertised, explaining what to do,
and giving options for how to do it regarding the services under contract. The goal
of customer training is to transfer the product or service developer's knowledge
about current and future applications to a particular customer.

In this activity, participants will analyze and discuss two interrelated perspectives
on customer training presented in the Discussion Starter Handout in order to
develop a foundation of knowledge that they'll use in the session to identify
customer training opportunities at this company.

● AGENDA

Step	Time
Step	*Time*
Discuss examples in the Discussion Starter Handout	15 minutes
Analyze examples from the workplace	10 minutes
Describe current and desired practices in the workplace	20 minutes
Wrap up	10 minutes

● INTRODUCTION

1. As participants enter the room, distribute copies of the Discussion Starter Handout and ask them to read it.

2. Begin the session by introducing the topic and why it's important:

> "We're here today to talk about customer training, a business strategy that is sometimes overlooked. It is different from customer service training, which tends to focus on the soft skills of interaction. Customer training, on the other hand, involves teaching customers the hard skills they need to make products work as advertised, explaining what to do, giving options regarding the services under contract, and transferring the product or service developer's knowledge about future applications to a particular customer. Customer training is a business deal that intends to give customers the skills and knowledge edge to truly understand the benefits of doing business with a company so that the customer considers that company the supplier of choice who understands their needs.

> "Customer trainers talk business, not education. Customer training is intensely focused on what the customer has recently purchased from your company. Customer training concentrates on what the customer intends to do with your product or service in order to enhance the customer's bottom line. It is training customized to a particular customer and to specific products or services purchased from you. It is 'win-win' training whose goal is to enable and empower your customer and contribute to your customer's profitability as well as to yours.

"The handout you received has two interrelated perspectives on customer service, a short list of typical ways to measure customers and some strategic elements of the job description of a customer trainer. If you haven't read the handout yet, please do so now."

● AWARENESS

3. After allowing several minutes for everyone to read and reflect on the handout, lead a discussion about the two parts, typical customer measures and items from the job description. Focus the discussion on participants' experiences with either kind of perspective. Ask participants to refer to the handout as the discussion continues. The following questions can be used to help guide this discussion:

   - Which of the typical customer measures do you use?

   - What do these customer measures that you use do for you (for example, make my performance review better, help me meet sales quotas, provide background information for public relations, and so on)?

   - How often are these customer measures updated in this company?

   - Who in this company is the point person for getting customer information?

   - Where does customer information reside? Is it accessible to everyone?

   - As you look at the job description, can you see how customer training can affect the typical customer measures and improve them? Which ones?

   - Have you ever been on the receiving end of customer training?

   - If yes, what effect did it have on your relationship with the provider of that product or service?

   - If no, would you have liked training in order to do your job better? What kind of training did you expect as a new customer?

   - Have you ever been a customer trainer? If yes, what were some of your objectives for that training and how did you measure success?

   Point out to the group that typical customer measures are enhanced by customer training.

● EXAMPLES

4. Explain to the group that they'll next examine the customer trainer job description more carefully as an example from the workplace. Introduce this specific job description by giving the group some background information about the company that employed customer trainers. The job description in the Discussion Starter Handout is from a company that sold chemical process simulators to customers around the globe. Training those specific customers to use the product to meet their particular business needs was a key commitment and business strategy of this company. The customer training manager reported jointly to the VP of sales and marketing and the VP of operations. In this company, customer training was a vital lifeline to the bottom line. The customer training function was never considered human resources or educational psychology; it was pure business, using teaching and learning as the means to help both companies fulfill their potentials.

5. Ask the group to refer to the Discussion Starter Handout's quote from the job description. Ask them what features of that particular customer training and that customer training manager's job seem like the best ideas.

● DEFINITION

6. Ask the group to focus now on their own organization, referring to the two perspectives in the Discussion Starter Handout as they define customer training opportunities at this company. Challenge participants to describe how customer learning can help this provider company become as great as it can be.

Ask them first to define the company's most successful products or services. Refer the group to the Typical Customer Measures listed on the Discussion Starter Handout. Ask the group to pick out any of those typical customer measures (number of new customers, percentage of market represented by this customer, or another one) that apply to this company's successes they've just defined. Get them thinking about the variety of ways to measure and describe customers.

Now turn their attention to the Items from Job Description of a Customer Training Manager on the Discussion Starter Handout. Ask them to pay particular attention to the emphasis on marketing—an emphasis not usually a part of a training manager's responsibilities. Note also the direction of growth responsibility. This training manager had to be a strategic thinker about the business possibilities in providing not only product and service but also training. Ask whether anyone can imagine ways in which customer training can respond to your own company's strategic growth initiatives.

7. Use the flip chart to record participants' responses or ask for a volunteer to act as scribe while you continue to facilitate discussion. For this definition, simply make a list of customer training opportunities here at this company—ones that are currently being implemented, and especially ones that no one has thought of yet. Start with having in mind a particular product or service that this company has created, and identify its customers. Ask the group, "What products or services here could benefit from strategic customer training?"

Record responses, list style, on the flip chart. Encourage participants to share their ideas with the group, leading into discussion about the importance of customer training and its potential for improving the bottom line at this company. Make the point that the power of customer training should not be underestimated nor implemented without careful, strategic planning connecting business goals with the typical measures of customer strength.

● WRAP UP

8. As a wrap-up activity, ask participants to think for a few minutes about how to deliver customer training. Lead a 10-minute discussion. Ask them to consider these things:

- Which customers should be trained? Decision makers or rank and file?

- Who should come first?

- What kinds of training delivery do you suggest?

- Is there a role for online training? What kind?

- Is there a role for coaching and other on-the-job customer training?

- Who should be entitled to this kind of one-to-one approach?

- Should customer training be "free" or built into the price of a product or service?

- What do you believe the correct, most effective reporting relationship should be for the customer training manager?

9. Distribute a copy of the Self-Examination, Reflection, and Action Planning Handout to each participant and explain that it can be used as a worksheet on the job.

HANDOUT 9.1
DISCUSSION STARTER HANDOUT FOR
Customer Training

Two Interrelated Perspectives

Typical Customer Measures

- Number of new customers

- Number of current and former customers retained

- Percentage of the market represented by this customer

- Percentage of corporate profitability or margin represented by this customer

- Customer satisfaction

- Demographic characteristics of customers

Items from Job Description of a Customer Training Manager

"Responsible for planning, marketing, design, development, and implementation of training programs supplied to clients with simulator and control system products. . . . Specific duties include:

- Analyze markets for training

- Initiate new training programs in response to company's direction of growth

- Coordinate training marketing efforts with total company marketing. . . ."

HANDOUT 9.2

SELF-EXAMINATION, REFLECTION, AND ACTION PLANNING HANDOUT FOR
Customer Training

∙∙

Self-Examination

The variety in the examples from the *Lunch and Learn* session should spark your imagination about what you personally can do to become a learning source for your customers. Think of yourself as a business planner and an instructional designer, one who analyzes the particular needs of particular customers for the kinds of learning that will have an impact on the central customer measures of customer acquisition, retention, profitability, satisfaction, and gaining market share. Take a look again at the elements of the job description in the Discussion Starter Handout as you think strategically.

Reflection

Think in terms of which measures you can directly or indirectly affect, and of the tools, media, or processes you'll choose to make your mark as a customer trainer. Identify customers on whom to focus. Think about your own availability, accessibility, flexibility, and listening and feedback skills. Share your ideas with others in the company whose work also has an effect on your customers. Choose persons anywhere in the company with whom you can collaborate in designing or delivering strategic customer training—training tied directly to the bottom line.

Action Planning

Document the good ideas you have for customer training as a strategy for success— that is, success defined by increased numbers in any of the typical customer measures listed on the Discussion Starter Handout. Identify other persons in your immediate team or work group, or outside of your normal work colleagues, with whom you might like to collaborate in designing or delivering training to customers. Keep a journal of customer training opportunities that you can identify as you interact with your customers. Define at least three action items of customer training that you could develop in order to serve customers better and yourself as well.

Performance

10
· · · · · · · ·

Change
· ·

Are you ready for your next job?

● PURPOSE

The big picture of occupational groups in the United States is changing: being prepared for career change is important to the health of individuals and to companies. The purpose of this session is to define changes in occupational groupings and the effects of these changes on individual workers.

● SUMMARY

Global, societal, corporate, and personal causes suggest a picture of where American workers will work in coming years. In this activity, participants will discuss the projections in the Discussion Starter Handout. These projections reflect the global changes that outsourcing is bringing, present a picture of a society stagnant in core occupational groups that we think of as the building blocks of America, suggest where corporate growth will occur, and give individuals a heads up on what kinds of jobs will await them in 2010. Then participants will define the effects of change in their work lives and prepare to take action to deal with change.

● AGENDA

Step	Time
Discuss the table in the Discussion Starter Handout	15 minutes
Provide examples from the workplace	15 minutes
Describe current and desired effects of workplace change	15 minutes
Wrap up	10 minutes

● INTRODUCTION

1. As participants enter the room, distribute copies of the Discussion Starter Handout and ask them to read it. Allow about 5 minutes for this, encouraging them to pay close attention to the big differences in the top five occupations listed and the bottom five listed. Encourage participants to think analytically and to compare the percentages.

2. Begin the session by introducing the topic and why it's important. Write the words *global, societal, corporate,* and *personal* on the flip chart. Direct participants' attention to them as you begin introducing the topic:

   "Today's session deals with the big picture of occupational change predicted to occur by the year 2010. Forces driving change include global and societal ones as well as corporate and personal ones. Understanding these forces is important as individuals and families try to make sense of national and international news and workforce trends, and as they plan where to live, how much to save for educational expenses, where to work, and how to plan for their future.

   "The table in the Discussion Starter Handout is from a larger report by the U.S. government's Bureau of Labor Statistics. Please refer to it now. Notice that the five occupations listed at the top of the table are involved with ideas and personal relationships and that the bottom five occupations listed are involved with handling or making things. We sometimes hear the first group characterized as occupations requiring 'knowledge' workers generally having education beyond high school. The second group of low-change occupations are generally thought of as core occupations that traditionally are considered the building blocks of America. This group of occupations—those of little change—does not necessarily require education beyond high school, and in fact, this group typically provides employment for many persons who have not completed high school. We sometimes contrast these groups as 'white collar' and 'blue collar.' These projections reflect the global changes that outsourcing is bringing, present a picture of a society stagnant in core occupational groups that we think of as the building blocks of America, suggest where corporate growth will occur, and give individuals a heads up on what kinds of jobs will await them in 2010."

● AWARENESS

3. Facilitate a discussion about the projections in the BLS chart. Start by asking these questions:

    • How many in this session today find themselves in one of these ten occupations? (Ask for a show of hands.)

    • Do you agree with what is reported here? Why or why not? Can you elaborate on your current situation?

    • How would you describe today's picture of your occupational category, and within it your own job?

● EXAMPLES

4. Referring to the four words written earlier on the flip chart, ask participants to first consider the "global" and "societal" causes or related trends that have an impact on their jobs. Ask for a volunteer scribe to record ideas on another flip chart so that participants can see both flip charts. Help the discussion to focus by suggesting any of the following ideas:

    • Low-cost labor overseas

    • Inexpensive and fast Internet and Web communication around the world

    • Increased competition for consumers everywhere in the world

    • Degradation and loss of U.S. manufacturing infrastructure

    • Better tax incentives offshore

    • Availability and reliability of low-wage workers in the United States

    Keep the discussion focused on the global and societal issues and trends that currently or in the near future affect participants' jobs and this workplace.

5. Now turn their attention to the words "corporate" and "personal" on the first flip chart. Ask participants to now consider causes and trends in these areas. Get them started in discussion with the following ideas. Continue recording on the second flip chart.

- Outsourcing
- Minimum wage
- Reduced benefits
- Aging workforce
- Immigrants

- Online certifications and advanced degrees
- Executive perks
- Bonus
- Knowledge-intensive economy
- Failing schools

● DEFINITION

6. Ask them now to share with the group how one or more of these causes or trends affect them personally in the way they do their work. Aim to find several specific examples from this workplace in each of the four categories.

7. Ask them if they've seen a difference in these effects during the time they've been employed at this company. Probe individual responses for specifics, both positive and negative. Keep discussion going for about 10 minutes.

8. Ask respondents whether they've seen an acceleration of change during their employment; if yes, ask them how they've changed the way they work to accommodate this change. Ask them if these changes are desirable changes. If not, ask them to elaborate on the status quo, on work slowdown, plant closings, or on deceleration of any kind and how they are affected by it.

● WRAP UP

9. To close the session, suggest that participants' work lives are impacted by change and that their effective responses to change depend on thoughtful consideration of opportunities in the areas of growth and actions to take to soften the blow of downward trends.

10. Tell participants that the handout you are about to give them can be a helpful tool as they define their own relationships to change and develop a plan of action to deal with it. Distribute the Self-Examination, Reflection, and Action Planning Handout.

HANDOUT 10.1

DISCUSSION STARTER HANDOUT FOR

Change

• •

Bureau of Labor Statistics (BLS) Percent Change Chart, Year 2010

This information is presented in descending order of projected percent increase, most change to least change.

Projected Employment by Major Occupational Group
(Percent Change from 2000 to 2010)

Professional and related occupations	18.4% change
Service occupations	17.9% change
Office and administrative support occupations	16.4% change
Management, business, and financial occupations	10.7% change
Sales and related occupations	10.7% change

++++++++++

Production occupations	9.0% change
Transportation and material moving occupations	6.9% change
Construction and extraction occupations	5.1% change
Installation, maintenance, and repair occupations	4.0% change
Farming, fishing, and forestry occupations	1.0% change

Source: www.bls.gov/news.release/ecopro

SELF-EXAMINATION, REFLECTION, AND ACTION PLANNING HANDOUT FOR

Change

· ·

Self-Examination and Reflection

Remember these four words as you think about change in your job in this company:

Global   **Societal**   **Corporate**   **Personal**

Think about the players and influences on change that affect you. Think about personal experience with change in the recent past and about personal challenges regarding change between now and the decade's end. Using the mental stimulation of the preceding discussion, define an area of your work life or personal life in which you can identify a recent change or can see a change coming in the future. Reflect on the nature of change for the greater good of organizations, corporations, communities, or families; define how you personally can become more empowered by understanding the change and operating effectively within it.

Action Planning

Begin to make a plan, identifying timelines, personal contacts, and resources you'll need for effective action. Resolve to be in charge of change. Here are some avenues for action:

- Political action

- Career development in your present job

- Retraining for different jobs

- Collaboration to conserve resources

11

• • • • • • • •

Ethics

• •

Do the right things right

● **PURPOSE**

Workplace ethics has to be more than moralizing from the main office. In order to build trust, workplace ethics must be demonstrated in consistent action throughout the workplace and in all business relationships. The purpose of this session is to define ethical behaviors in this workplace.

● **SUMMARY**

Workplace ethics include employee relationships, customer relationships, supplier relationships, shareholder relationships, community relationships, and others. Ethical conduct involves both heart and head, responsibility, commitment, and standards. In this activity, participants will analyze the definition of "ethical behavior" contained in the *Baldrige National Quality Program Criteria for Performance Excellence* (2004) and relate their work to it. In this analysis, they will be guided by the Native American "Circle of Life" and its foundations of ethical behavior from this culture.

● AGENDA

Step	Time
Discuss the graphic in the Discussion Starter (A) Handout	10 minutes
Discuss the reference in Discussion Starter (B) Handout	10 minutes
Provide examples from the workplace	15 minutes
Describe current and desired practices in the workplace	10 minutes
Wrap up	10 minutes

● INTRODUCTION

1. As participants enter the room, distribute copies of the Discussion Starter (A) Handout (The Circle of Life) and the Discussion Starter (B) Handout (Baldrige Explanation of Ethical Behavior). (If you prefer, you can make a two-sided copy for each participant, A on one side and B on the other, so that each person has only once piece of paper to deal with.)

2. Begin the session by introducing the topic and why it's important from a personal perspective and from a business perspective.

3. Refer participants first to the Circle of Life Handout and ask them to notice the features of the Circle of Life, including the feathers in the center. Use this graphic to help participants focus on the personal characteristics of ethical behavior. Ask them what they see in the Circle of Life. Then continue with the following observations:

   "When people behave ethically, their actions are described by words such as truthful, accountable, consistent, focused, disciplined, humble, patient, compassionate, discerning, inclusive. The Circle of Life is found in many countries and cultures, including Native American culture. The image of persons reaching out to and connected with each other in a circle is a representation of an ancient and contemporary belief that we are all related in common pursuit. The Africans' circle of life, the great stone circles of Europe, the mandalas of India, and the medicine wheels of America's Chippewa Indians serve as a unifying and empowering symbol of humanity's quest to avoid suffering, live in harmony, and be happy. The addition of the eagle feathers in the center of the circle reminds us to relentlessly search—to be eagle-eyed—for justice and right relationships. With carefully placed stones in meaningful patterns within a circle in the grass, Chippewa Native Americans focused on qualities such as purity, clarity, wisdom, illumination, strength, trust, and love, and on processes such as introspection, cleansing, and renewal, certainly some of the foundations of what we today consider ethical behavior today.

"But the definition of ethical behavior often eludes us. We confuse what seems right at the moment in a certain context with what is surely wrong in the long run; we develop our intellectual selves to the exclusion of or with imbalance of our spiritual selves. We let anger, fear, and greed block our positive impact on others. We are not sure that corporate values are played out in ethical behavior in the corporation. We remain silent when we should speak. We forget the notion of personal responsibility and lose touch with opportunities for service for the good of all. We abandon the circle.

"Now turn to the Discussion Starter (B) Handout and read the explanation of the U.S. government's National Institute of Standards and Technology's concept and practice of ethical behavior."

● AWARENESS

4. Allow several minutes for participants to read the excerpt from the *Baldrige Criteria*. Guide participants' thinking to the organizational issues raised in the excerpt. As they are reading, go to a flip chart and write on it the following words from the Baldrige excerpt:

- Behavior

- Moral and professional principles

- Right from wrong

- Role models

- Communicated

- Reinforced

- Mission and vision aligned

- Empower

5. Lead participants through the list of words, one by one, and ask whether they agree with the statements on the handout. Ask them to modify any of those words according to their own understanding or experience. Keep the focus on organizations as participants elaborate on the excerpt.

6. Now bring the two sides of the Discussion Starter Handout together by suggesting that A deals mainly with personal characteristics and B deals mainly with organizational concepts. Both are necessary for ethical workplace behavior.

● EXAMPLES

7. Facilitate a discussion of examples of unethical behavior. Start participants off by suggesting several common problems: stealing supplies, back-dating paperwork, calling in sick when you're not sick, breaking confidence, changing the rules mid-stream, withholding information, and so on. Help participants understand what ethical behavior is by stating what it is not.

8. Conclude this exercise by asking participants to reverse their thinking and turn these unethical behaviors they've just heard into positive statements of what ethical behavior is. Remind them that they should think in terms of behaviors—actions—and help them start each statement with an action word. Record their statements on a flip chart. Aim for at least five statements.

● DEFINITION

9. Using the examples of ethical behavior just recorded on the flip chart, ask the group to connect the underlying ideas and make a narrative definition of ethical behavior in this workplace. Ask for a volunteer scribe to work at the flip chart to write the definition of ethical behavior at this workplace. Continue facilitating discussion until all ideas have surfaced and the statement is clearly presented.

10. Here are some examples of how a company can demonstrate ethical behavior. Use these to encourage a deeper examination of the ways in which ethical behavior improves work. Compare these with the definition above. Modify the definition above to include any of these ideas.

   • Supervisors care about employee well-being.

   • Employees here are encouraged to make changes to improve the work that they do.

- The company encourages and enables employees to develop job skills so they can advance their careers.

- We have a safe work environment.

- Employees are thanked and recognized for their contributions.

● WRAP UP

11. Close the session by reiterating the positive examples and behaviors in this company. Refer back to the two Discussion Starter Handouts, which suggest personal as well as organizational responsibilities regarding ethical behavior.

12. Distribute a copy of the Self-Examination, Reflection, and Action Planning Handout to each participant and explain that participants can use this worksheet to help organize their thoughts as they fine-tune their definitions and demonstrations of ethical workplace behavior.

REFERENCE

Baldrige National Quality Program 2004 Criteria for Performance Excellence. (2004). Gaithersburg, MD: National Institute of Standards and Technology.

DISCUSSION STARTER (A) HANDOUT FOR
Ethics

Circle of Life

HANDOUT 11.2
DISCUSSION STARTER (B) HANDOUT FOR
Ethics*

• •

Baldrige Explanation of Ethical Behavior

The term "ethical behavior" refers to how an organization ensures that all its decisions, actions, and stakeholder interactions conform to the organization's moral and professional principles. These principles are the foundation for the organization's culture and values, and they differentiate "right" from "wrong."

Senior leaders should act as role models for these principles of behavior. The principles apply to all individuals involved in the organization, from employees to members of the board of directors, and need to be communicated and reinforced on a regular basis. Although there is no universal model for ethical behavior, senior leaders should ensure that the organization's mission and vision are aligned with its ethical principles. Ethical behavior should be practiced with all stakeholders, including employees, shareholders, customers, partners, suppliers, and the organization's local community.

While some organizations may view their ethical principles as boundary conditions restricting behavior, well-designed and clearly articulated ethical principles should empower people to make effective decisions with great confidence.

*Source: Glossary of Key Terms, *Baldrige National Quality Program 2004 Criteria for Performance Excellence*, 2004, Gaithersburg, MD: National Institute of Standards and Technology (NIST), p. 30.

HANDOUT 11.3

SELF-EXAMINATION, REFLECTION, AND ACTION PLANNING HANDOUT FOR

Ethics

• •

Self-Examination

We know intuitively that the state of our mind and heart together allows ethical content of our behavior to develop and drives our ethical behavior to keep growing and improving. Keep this list of personal descriptors of ethical behavior, introduced earlier in the *Lunch and Learn* session, as a daily reminder of desirable characteristics:

- Truthful
- Accountable
- Consistent
- Focused
- Disciplined

- Humble
- Patient
- Compassionate
- Discerning
- Inclusive

Reflection

The business press during the first half of the first decade of the new millennium has been full of corporate scandals and ethical shortcomings: the names Fastow, Skilling, Ebbers, Grasso, and Stewart have raised our collective consciousness about ethics and what drives our values. Reflect on these examples and try to identify the ethical problems they represented.

Action Planning

Resolve to act in ethical ways to correct the wrongs and move forward with the rights as you see them in your organization. Keep a checklist or journal to record your actions.

12

·········

Goals

·······································

What gets counted, gets done

● PURPOSE

Setting and reaching goals keeps a business moving forward. The purpose of this session is to study the nature of goals and to develop a mental framework for meeting them.

● SUMMARY

One of the most important things about goals is that they can be measured. If goals are so idealistic or unrealistic that they can't be measured, they are hollow words and ineffective in driving positive change. In this activity, participants will take a hard look at goals and the kinds of measurements associated with them. They will leave this session more aware and better able to set and achieve their own personal and organizational goals.

● AGENDA

Step	Time
Discuss the goal in the Discussion Starter Handout	15 minutes
Provide examples of personal or organizational goals	15 minutes
Describe current and desired practices in the workplace	15 minutes
Wrap up	10 minutes

● INTRODUCTION

1. As participants enter the room, distribute copies of the Discussion Starter Handout and ask them to read it.

2. Begin the session by introducing the topic and why it's important. Write the following words on a flip chart: *important, plausible, measurable, simply stated.*

   "Success doesn't happen just because you want it to happen. It's working toward goals and reaching them that tells the story of productivity, sales success, achievement, and personal empowerment. This means that things are counted and analyzed as work occurs and as jobs are completed. It also means that motivations, accountabilities, and supports are in place to help along the way.

   "The handout you received contains a simple statement of a goal—a weight-loss goal. It's an example of an important goal, a goal that is plausible, one that can be measured, and is stated unambiguously in easy-to-understand language. The bullet items below the goal statement suggest some of the dimensions of working toward that goal. Take a few seconds to read the goal and the six bullet points; if you are not familiar with the organizations listed, check with one of your teammates in this session who seems to know what they are. [Allow a few minutes for questioning.]

   "As we talk about this particular goal in the Discussion Starter Handout, pay attention to the kinds of measurements that each of those six bullet items suggests, and to the kinds of supports built into those programs that potentially facilitate reaching the weight-loss goal. In about 15 minutes, we'll relate those kinds of measurements and supports to goals here in our teams and organizations."

3. Begin a discussion about this weight-loss goal, referring to the four terms on the flip chart. Ask participants how many have been involved in a serious weight-loss program themselves. After a show of hands, focus on those folks as you facilitate discussion about how they measured their progress in working toward their own personal goals. Ask for a volunteer to act as scribe at the flip chart as participants' comments are made.

4. Get them started by writing several kinds of measurements on the flip chart; for example, choose two or three from this list, asking participants for other kinds of measurements:

- Carbs counted

- Calories counted

- Pounds recorded on a scale

- Inches recorded using a tape measure

- Frequency of attendance at meetings

- Cholesterol reading improvements

- Incidence of praise from fellow dieters

- Exercise schedules kept

- Clothing size reduced

5. Make the point that these measurements support the goal and increase accountability. Goals at work need to be stated in similar simple terms with measurement indicators that relate to accomplishing those goals.

6. Conclude this discussion about weight-loss goals by asking participants to share with the group some of the measurements that worked for them, as well as any goal-setting and planning techniques that they found helpful. Make the point that goals need to be more than platitudes, and measurements need to be monitored in a way that means something to the goal seeker.

7. Make a transition to team and organizational goals by introducing the idea of "know thyself" and its critical role in identifying the supports one needs in order to set realistic goals. Refer back to the flip chart with the four terms: *important, plausible, measurable, simply stated.* Suggest that we all start from different places as we embark on working toward goals, and that we all need

different kinds of support. Ask the group what some of their personal quirks and preferences are for support during dieting. Start them off with any of these suggestions:

- I like to diet with a buddy.

- I can't stand hype and "happy talk" from weight loss leaders, so I'll need to check out and compare Jenny Craig with Weight Watchers and other similar programs to find the best fit for me.

- Constraints of preparing food for the rest of the family sometimes annoy me.

- I'll need to be sure the diet and exercise centers are not so far away from my home or office that I use distance as an excuse for poor attendance.

In short, individuals need to analyze their own psychological needs, identify the supports available to them, and make a plan to work toward achieving a goal—a plan "that works for me."

● EXAMPLES

8. Now shift attention away from weight-loss goals and move on to discussion around defining goals in their work lives. Suggest that they choose either a productivity goal or a relationship goal at work. Examples can be a personal individual goal or a team or organizational goal. As participants try to come up with a simple yet important goal, plausible and measurable, suggest that high-performing individuals are often considered a company's greatest asset. Ask participants to be specific, stating just one goal to share with the group. Record these on a flip chart.

9. After you have a good, representative list from the group, go through the goals one by one and ask the group what the payoffs are (or were) for accomplishing each one. Allow about 15 minutes for discussion.

● DEFINITION

10. Ask the group to look at this list of goals to try to see commonalities among them. Help them to focus on the different kinds of measurements that are needed for this list of goals at this company. For example, a group of the goals might be measurable by time indicators; some might be measurable

by incidence of error; some by numbers of personnel, frequency of career moves, amount of litigation, and so on. Encourage participants to take a hard look at this list of goals and state a descriptive definition of "goals at this company" based on what they see written here on the flip charts. Allow about 15 minutes for this discussion.

● WRAP UP

11. To close the session, review the four terms on the first flip-chart page: *important*, *plausible*, *measurable*, and *simply stated*. Encourage participants to set goals that can be met, to monitor progress toward accomplishment, to evaluate results of efforts, and to take action to make changes.

12. Tell participants that getting in the habit of self-examination and reflection about progress toward their goals will make it easier to reach those goals.

13. Distribute a copy of the Self-Examination, Reflection, and Action Planning Handout to each participant and suggest that participants can use this worksheet to set and achieve their goals.

DISCUSSION STARTER HANDOUT FOR
Goals

·· ··· ···

"from 175 pounds to 150 pounds by April 30"

- Atkins

- Jenny Craig

- South Beach Diet

- Weight Watchers

- Curves for Women

- Swimming at the YMCA

SELF-EXAMINATION, REFLECTION, AND ACTION PLANNING HANDOUT FOR
Goals

• •

Self-Examination

As you recall the discussion about weight loss and the characteristics of that goal, think about similar goal statements in your individual job, your team's growth or future focus, and your boss's and board's corporate goals as they affect you. In each setting, ask yourself these four critical questions that have a large impact on whether or not a goal ever can be accomplished:

• Is the goal *important*? To me? To my supervisor? To stockholders?

• Is the goal *plausible*? That is, can it be achieved? Or is it just fancy words?

• Is the goal *measurable*? Can I see clearly how to measure progress toward it?

• Is the goal *simply stated*? Can I personally understand it?

Reflection

Reflect on some of the goals stated in this session, especially on the ones that perhaps don't meet the four standards above. Think about ways in which to define those goals better; choose words that motivate and lead to accomplishment.

Action Planning

Think in terms of obstacles to your ability to meet goals; include actions to overcome obstacles or to prevent barriers from being constructed. Consider communication problems and problems with the way things are done. Resolve to be a supporter of others as you journey together in meeting individual and organizational goals.

13
·······

Priorities

··

First things first

● PURPOSE

Employees from company leaders on down need to do the kind of work that makes a positive contribution to life at work and in the larger economy. The purpose of this session is to examine an example from the press and examples from this company to clarify an approach to putting first things first.

● SUMMARY

Performance based on priorities is the kind of work most of us want to do. Yet, we don't often take the time to set priorities in order to do the work that matters most. In this activity, participants will look at various dimensions of setting priorities and suggest several priorities for their own work that can ultimately lead to improved performance.

● AGENDA

Step	Time
Discuss examples in the Discussion Starter Handout	15 minutes
Provide examples from the workplace	15 minutes
Describe current and desired practices in this workplace	15 minutes
Wrap up	10 minutes

● INTRODUCTION

1. As participants enter the room, distribute copies of the Discussion Starter Handout and ask them to read it.

2. Begin the session by introducing the topic and why it's important:

   "We're here today to talk about setting priorities as individuals and as a company. The choices we make as employees and company representatives affect operations and relationships, and, of course, profit. We look to our leaders to help us set priorities and be examples to us by their actions. We are angry and confused at press coverage of high-profile CEOs and their apparent mistakes. We want to make honest, legal, appropriate decisions.

   "But sometimes the choices we make are questionable and lead to trouble. Performance based on priorities is the kind of work most of us want to do. Yet, we don't often take the time to set priorities in order to do the work that matters most. In this activity, you'll look at various dimensions of setting priorities and will suggest several priorities for your own work that can ultimately lead to improved performance and contributions to the company's success.

   "The handout you received has an example of priorities that have been questioned. The brief narrative is followed by five questions that will focus your thinking on priorities. If you've not already done so, please read the example now and think about your answers to those questions."

● AWARENESS

3. As participants are reading the handout, write these words on a flip chart to guide discussion of the example:

- Accountability

- Transparency

- Disclosure

- Leadership

- Performance

4. After allowing 1 or 2 minutes for everyone to read the handout, lead a discussion about the example, using the words you've just written on the flip chart to guide you. The following questions can help facilitate discussion:

- In the case of the New York Stock Exchange, do you fault the directors?

- What do you believe happens in an organization that allows executive privilege to get so out of hand?

- What does pay for performance mean? What should it mean?

- What should have been the Stock Exchange's compensation priorities?

- What should have been the leadership priorities?

● EXAMPLES

5. Now ask the group to focus on this company and its priorities in any area of work: process, product, relationships, training, employee development, finance, sales, shareholder and board activities, marketing, contracting, leadership, and so on. Ask them to identify some examples of obvious company priorities in any area they can think of. Record their ideas on a flip chart, or ask for a volunteer from the group to act as scribe. At this point, don't try to organize or categorize their ideas; aim for a variety of examples from the company.

● DEFINITION

6. Now ask the group to think about what values these priorities suggest. Ask participants whether they believe the priorities that have been in evidence through actions they've observed and that they have been part of are the "right" ones. Aim for clarification and alignment of values and priorities.

7. If you've uncovered some misalignment or problems with the priorities in evidence, ask the group to make specific suggestions for improvement. Ask them to focus on what they, individually, can do in order to make organizational improvements that help define correct priorities. Here are some ideas. Suggest any or all of these to get discussion going:

   - Inspiring others to higher performance

   - Facilitating more effective relationships

   - Partnering and collaborating to get work done

   - Counseling

   - Helping people help themselves

   - Coaching

   - Sharing information

   - Enhancing and developing resources

   - Confronting criticism

   - Resolving conflict

   All these and more are things that ordinary people at work can do. Performance that is based on the right priorities is the real deal.

● WRAP UP

8. To close the session, ask the group what seem to be the most obvious good priorities of this company—the ones that have the best effect on high performance. Put a star or checkmark next to those on any of the flip chart pages you've created earlier in the session. Reaffirm that these priorities are worth working for.

9. Tell participants that additional self-examination, reflection, and action planning will help them to apply what they've learned in this session to their jobs and their performance.

10. Refer them back to the Discussion Starter Handout and the questions. Urge participants to not be afraid to ask tough questions when it comes to priorities in evidence in their organizations and in this company.

11. Distribute a copy of the Self-Examination, Reflection, and Action Planning Handout to each participant and explain that they can use this back on the job to organize their thoughts and questions.

HANDOUT 13.1

DISCUSSION STARTER HANDOUT FOR
Priorities

• •

Let's Talk Priorities . . .

The former head of the New York Stock Exchange, Richard A. Grasso, caused a huge public outcry when his excessive compensation package was investigated by New York state's Attorney General Eliot Spitzer. Grasso was forced to resign in September 2003 when his board asked for his resignation. The case raised the level of discussion about executive pay, board irresponsibility, pursuit of personal gain, and abuse of information.

Much of Mr. Grasso's "golden parachute" was undisclosed until after he retired as chairman of the New York Stock Exchange. He left the Exchange with a $139.5 million retirement and severance package that was in dispute many months after his departure.*

Questions

How did leadership go so terribly wrong?

Whatever happened to transparency? Where does it fit?

Is competition for top jobs worth this price?

Which comes first, legal or ethical?

What are the priorities in pay for performance?

Are CEOs of non-profit organizations held to higher standards?

*Source: "Mayday? Payday! Hit the Silk!" by Timothy L. O'Brien in *The New York Times,* Sunday business section, January 9, 2005, p. 6.

SELF-EXAMINATION, REFLECTION, AND ACTION PLANNING HANDOUT FOR
Priorities

. . . .

Self-Examination

Resolve today to be a leader in terms of performance based on priorities. Examine your own actions within the areas you consider priorities in your job. Identify several priority areas in which you personally can be an effective and facilitative leader or simply a more successful performer. Write down your ideas for later reference as you do your work.

-

-

-

-

Reflection

Reflect on the needs of the company that were identified in the *Lunch and Learn* session and how you might have contributed to both the problems and the solutions. Reflect on your own role in setting priorities, and in changing priorities for the good of the company.

Action Planning

Develop a simple system or set of guidelines for action that propels you forward to better performance. Consider also leadership—the kind of leadership that occurs regardless of level or job title, the kind of leadership that simply has followers. Focus on the right priorities and your own highly personal direction for action within those priorities.

14

·········

Recognition and Rewards

··

There's power in "please"
and "thank you"

● PURPOSE

Recognition and rewards are known to keep employees happy, productive, and loyal and are appreciated by those who receive them. The purpose of this session is to examine the reasons for and characteristics of various kinds of recognition and rewards and to choose those that would be most likely to motivate and reward people at work.

● SUMMARY

Giving recognition and rewards to employees is a common practice in many organizations. In this activity, participants will consider recognition and rewards in this and in other companies and will suggest the recognition and rewards that are most appropriate and effective for their own work.

● AGENDA

Step	Time
Discuss symbols in the Discussion Starter Handout	15 minutes
Provide examples from the workplace	15 minutes
Describe current and desired practices in the workplace	15 minutes
Wrap up	10 minutes

● INTRODUCTION

1. As participants enter the room, distribute copies of the Discussion Starter Handout and ask them to look at all of the symbols on it.

2. Begin the session by introducing the topic and why it's important:

   "We're here today to talk about recognition and rewards. Most of us have had some experience with recognition and rewards in our organizational lives. We earn points, accumulate checkmarks, earn bonuses, get stars for perfect attendance, and aim for those golf trophies in the corporate tournament. We devise various measurement systems to show that performance worthy of recognition and rewards has been demonstrated, and we believe that sincere recognition and meaningful rewards motivate us to perform better and to cement our loyalty to our companies. We believe that rewards for excellent behavior tend to reinforce that behavior so that it happens again. We like recognition and we work hard for rewards.

   "The handout you received contains five symbols associated with recognition and rewards. Please refer to the handout now as we talk about the experiences you've had with recognition and rewards and the ideas you have for making them work at this company."

3. With the handouts in front of participants, direct their attention to the four symbols on the periphery of the page: the checkmark, the star, the frequency tally, and the normal curve.

4. Suggest that these four symbols are typical ways of measuring achievement. Ask participants what their experiences have been with any or all of these symbols in measuring their own behaviors, and which ones are used in their organization. Help them review the processes in their organization and teams to focus on what goes into recognition. Suggest that these indicators applied to processes and products help to define the behaviors that are worthy of recognition and rewards. These are some of the kinds of responses participants might offer:

- I use checkmarks on grid paper to document what tasks I've completed.

- Our team uses a "star system" to recognize team members each Friday who demonstrated "out of the box" thinking that week. All team members vote on how many stars (1 to 5) the person being recognized should receive. We post the stars on a chart in the team captain's office.

- The sales department uses frequency counts to keep track of sales made within a two-week period. It's easy to see who's ahead and due to be recognized.

- Our quality guidelines say that we should aim for the two tails of the normal curve where the "Six Sigma" quality occurs. When we get there, we recognize the individuals who were the most helpful in meeting that high standard.

If participants can't think of any examples, use the four bullet points above to spark their memories. Turn them into questions, for example, "Have you ever used checkmarks on grid paper to document what tasks you've completed? Stars?" and so on.

● EXAMPLES

5. Now turn participants' attention to this particular company or team to iden-tify ways in which the company recognizes individuals for outstanding per-formance. Ask participants to give examples of things this company does to give recognition. Write the word "Recognition" at the top of the flip-chart page and record their responses, or ask someone from the group to act as scribe. Keep this activity focused on recognition only; you'll facilitate discussion of rewards separately.

6. To help them start, write one or two of these following typical items on the flip chart. Encourage participants to think broadly about places to look for evidence of recognition. Here are some examples of *recognition:*

   • Feature article in corporate newsletter

   • Photos in the board room

   • "Employee of the Week" designation on posters and website

   • Appointment to cross-functional team

   • Assignment as a mentor

   • Invitation to speak at a corporate conference or training workshop

   • Being on loan to a community group to share your expertise

7. Following the same procedure as Step 6, now turn participants' attention to *rewards.* Using another flip-chart page, write the word "Rewards" at the top, and continue. Encourage participants to think broadly about rewards, but refer them first to the set of twenty-dollar bills in the center of the Discussion Starter. Pose the question: "Are rewards always financial?" Try to help partici-pants to make a distinction between recognition and rewards. Introducing the financial foundation of most rewards might help them think more clearly about how to distinguish recognition from reward. Following are some typical *rewards;* use them to encourage responses from the group:

   • Increased budget for your project

   • Promotion

   • Increased company contribution to your retirement

   • Pay increase

- Super Bowl tickets

- Golf club membership

- Concert or theater tickets

- Caribbean cruise

- New laptop

- Coffee mug

8. After you've created the two lists, Recognition and Rewards, lead a discussion about the company culture that's reflected in these lists. Ask for opinions from participants about whether or not the recognition and rewards are effective and what they accomplish.

● DEFINITION

9. Now move into an exercise in which you ask participants to first discuss this company's recognition and rewards practices and then make a statement that defines this company's approach. Use a flip chart to record their ideas.

10. Compare the participants' statement of definition with the conventional wisdom about recognition and rewards. That is, that "recognition and rewards keep employees happy, productive, and loyal." Pay attention to variations of these results and to any other benefits that participants can identify at this company. Add a "Benefits" statement to the definition on the flip chart; list benefits as a bullet list on the flip chart.

11. Now ask the group by show of hands to vote for the benefits the group thinks have the biggest payoff for the company. Add any items to the examples flip-chart pages or to this definition page that the group would *like to see* at this company and vote on these extra ones too.

● WRAP UP

12. To close the session, ask participants to think about themselves as the giver of recognition and rewards as well as the receiver of them. Challenge them to be aware of the emotional boost that being appreciated can provide to corporate life, and challenge them to seek ways to make their own unique contributions as they interact with people on their own teams and across the company.

13. Distribute a copy of the Self-Examination, Reflection, and Action Planning Handout to each participant and explain that participants can use this as a worksheet as they engage in more meaningful and purposeful recognition and rewards processes.

14. Suggest that teams or work groups get together soon to review the recognition and rewards programs they currently use. Suggest that they focus on both the goals and the benefits, and make changes if change seems needed.

DISCUSSION STARTER HANDOUT FOR
Recognition and Rewards

SELF-EXAMINATION, REFLECTION, AND ACTION PLANNING HANDOUT FOR
Recognition and Rewards

· ·

Self-Examination

Consider your own personal feelings about some recognition and/or rewards that you have received. Make a chart, listing the recognition/rewards down the left side. Then make a brief comment, journal style, in the appropriate column about your own reactions to someone showing you appreciation.

Recognition/ Reward	I Felt Appreciation Because	I Did Not Feel Appreciation Because

Reflection

Reflect on the personal and organizational reasons why you feel the way you do, and resolve to take action to reinforce the good situations and correct the bad situations.

Action Planning

Use the analysis of your feelings about the recognition/rewards in the previous chart to commit to a plan of action to make your own work or that of someone else more meaningful and productive. Make a list of action items, or write a memo to yourself in narrative style. Focus on action and on benefits.

**Actions I can take regarding recognition and rewards
to increase appreciation and encourage meaningful work:**

Problem Solving

15

· · · · · · · ·

Conflict Management

· ·

"First feelings, second thoughts"
—Daniel Goleman

● PURPOSE

Recognizing issues, problems, and conflicts before they turn into crises is an important job function of employees at every level. The purpose of this session is to identify basic skills of conflict management from both the emotional and the cognitive points of view. The focus of the session is on fundamentals and some basic techniques of conflict management.

● SUMMARY

To be sure, every worker needs to develop skills of conflict management in order to have a comfortable, safe, and productive working environment. The basic skills of managing conflict are both emotional and cognitive, and in this session participants will examine both kinds of basic skills for conflict management. In this activity, participants will focus on areas in this company in which specific conflict management strategies should be developed and name these strategies. A basic plan for conflict management will be started.

● AGENDA

Step	Time
Step	*Time*
Discuss examples in the Discussion Starter Handout	10 minutes
Provide examples from the workplace	15 minutes
Describe current and desired practices in the workplace	15 minutes
Wrap up	15 minutes

● INTRODUCTION

1. As participants enter the room, distribute copies of the Discussion Starter Handout and ask them to study it, paying particular attention to the emotional focus, Drawing A at the top of the page, versus the cognitive focus, Drawing B at the bottom of the page.

2. Begin the session by introducing the topic and why it's important:

> "We're here today to talk about managing conflict. Workers everywhere, and especially people in leadership positions in teams or groups, must develop skills of conflict management in order to have comfortable, safe, and productive working relationships. The Discussion Starter Handout provides an example of two important conflict management approaches that come from different sides of our intelligence, the emotional side and the cognitive side.

> "You'll see that the Discussion Starter quotes Daniel Goleman, the best-selling author of books on emotional intelligence. Goleman's perspective is that emotions always come first in human relations, especially in problem solving and conflict management. All of the cognitive skills, or intelligence associated with cognition, follow the first burst of emotional intelligence about a situation. 'First feelings, second thoughts' is how he says it.

> "During the rest of this session, we'll explore the fundamental idea of a ladder of emotions and the basic technique of getting to win-win through carefully thought-out cognitive decisions. Together these two concepts, the ladder of emotions and the win-win decision, will provide some fundamental skill development techniques for conflict management."

● AWARENESS

3. Suggest that participants continue to focus on the Discussion Starter Handout. Explain Drawing A, the Ladder of Emotions, first. Guide participants' reading of the ladder from bottom to top. Explain that the top rung, fear, represents the strongest emotion of all rungs on the ladder. If one starts at the bottom with the emotion of confusion, as shown in the drawing, it soon becomes apparent that each higher rung represents an ever-stronger emotion. Taken together, the five successive rungs of the ladder combine to create the emotion of fear.

4. Now ask the group to choose another strong emotion. Some suggestions are anger, joy, sadness, or love. Ask for a participant volunteer to come to the flip chart and construct a similar ladder, putting the strong emotion chosen by the group at the top of the ladder. For example, if joy were chosen, some of the contributing rungs of the ladder might be satisfaction, contentment, and delight; if anger were chosen, some of the contributing rungs might be irritation, resentment, and hostility. Let the volunteer take over the flip-chart activity, constructing at least one Ladder of Emotions based on the group's contributions. Refer back to the Goleman quote, "First feelings, second thoughts," on the Discussion Starter Handout. The objective of this activity is to increase awareness of a range of emotions. Thank the volunteer, and ask that he or she return to the group. Suggest that dealing with the lower rungs of the ladder first can prevent the feelings at lower levels from escalating to the top.

5. Now switch focus to the bottom part of the handout, B, Think Win-Win. Guide the group's attention to the lower half of the handout featuring a crock of butter and a pat of butter wrapped in foil. Point out that they are now in the "second thoughts" part of the Goleman directive. Suggest to the group that the cognition involved here is decision making regarding which butter to choose, given certain circumstances. Conflict management involves choices in thinking as well as in dealing with emotions.

6. Read the following short story* to the group, telling them to listen for the win-win decision that illustrates a better way to think about the situation.

   "The German restaurant in the next town serves wonderful bread and warm rolls, on which customers like to pile fresh butter. The chef thinks that the customers' eyes are bigger than their stomachs and

---

*Source: Adapted from "Win-Win," in *Games That Drive Change* (pp. 265–266) by C. Nilson. New York: McGraw-Hill, 1995. Copyright © The McGraw-Hill Companies, Inc. Used with permission.

refuses to put out crocks of tempting butter because so much of it comes back to the kitchen and is wasted. Management is not pleased at the chef's action, thinks he is being stingy, and a conflict situation is set up.

"Think Win-Win is what now is needed. If the chef can wrap pats of butter in foil in generous individual servings and put the butter pats—plus a few extras—on the tables, the conflicting parties have demonstrated that they can think win-win. The customers can still indulge their butter urges and the chef doesn't waste what hasn't been opened. Management is happy. The solution is a win-win.

"This solution is more than a compromise. It is based on the technique of choosing what are the most important things to save out of the difficult situation; it's the idea of going above and beyond the current stalemate to introduce something new in the situation—in the case of the butter, the introduction of foil-wrapped pats. Compromise is most often seen as both sides giving in, or giving up something. Try to get in the habit of thinking win-win as you resolve the cognitive challenges to preserve what's best about a situation."

● EXAMPLES

7. Focus more specifically on your organization in this workplace. Try to think of examples from both ways of looking at problems, the emotional intelligence way and the cognitive intelligence way. A good place to start is to recall an escalating or high-rung example of emotions from your own work or your organization. Refer participants back to the ladders created a few minutes ago on the flip chart. Encourage them to find examples specific to this company.

8. Write their ideas on another flip chart and keep the flip charts side by side. Lead a discussion of the act of prioritizing the components of the emotion(s) they've identified; be prepared for some disagreement on the order of things. When there seems to be general agreement from the group, challenge them to explain what kinds of actions they'd take at each step of the ladder to recognize and begin to solve the emotional problem at each level before the levels compound to major conflict or even crisis stage. Before you leave this discussion, repeat the phrase, "First Feelings, Second Thoughts."

9. After participants have demonstrated some basic skills of emotional problem solving, turn their attention to the Think Win-Win example of the two ways to present the restaurant butter. Repeat the partial quote, ". . . Second Thoughts."

Remind them that thinking win-win, above and beyond, instead of compromise will help channel the cognitive intellectual skills they'll need to manage many conflict situations. Encourage the group to define some potential conflicts in their organizations. Use the bullet lists below to get them started with examples. Here are some ideas regarding individuals:

- Longer work week with no more pay

- Having to cover for jobs other than their own job

- Greater accountability and performance demands

- Lack of adequate security personnel

- Being overwhelmed by computer systems that are confusing and don't deliver

- Lack of recognition for doing a good job

Here are some ideas regarding the organization as a whole:

- Pattern of rapid turnover in the employee base

- Dwindling talent

- Loss of core business

- Competition from overseas cheap labor

- Rising costs of providing security

Suggest any of these ideas in order to stimulate participants to offer other suggestions that are potential hot spots in their organizations. Ask the group to choose one or two of the suggestions just given for further analysis.

● DEFINITION

10. Next, lead the group in a description of how to manage the specific challenges of this workplace, and remember, "First Feelings, Second Thoughts." Working with the suggestions from the group, begin by defining and prioritizing the emotions involved, and give a suggestion for creating a win-win situation

through effective decision making. Aim to help the group to think both emotionally and cognitively in solving or preventing the conflict situation they've identified.

Here's an example based on the emotion of anger. Note the conflict management elements of contributing emotions, and the "above and beyond" or new element introduced through a cognitive approach. Note the emotional as well as the cognitive foundations of the priority statements.

- *Priority 1:* Develop an anger management workshop with an online component accessible to any worker at any time.

- *Priority 2:* Communicate and carry out the policy regarding whistle blowing; include whistle blowing that involves escalating emotions such as suspicion and resentment.

- *Priority 3:* Take a look at all departments' performance review standards and guidelines for consistency and fairness. Publish an updated version of standards.

- *Priority 4:* Assign mentors or coaches right away when new employees, especially people from other countries and global partners, join the company to prevent anxiety from escalating.

Keep discussion going until the group has suggested several priorities. Ask a participant to act as scribe at the flip chart to write down the group's ideas.

● WRAP UP

11. Begin wrapping up this session by asking the group to focus for a few minutes on positive examples of conflict management in use at this company. Challenge them to think about positive conflict management examples from their own experiences with team members, customers, supervisors, and fellow workers. Facilitate discussion on evidence of examples of behaviors, actions, or systems at this company that demonstrate the positives in this company's ability to prevent or manage conflict. Encourage participants to think in terms of the benefits to the company of these positives.

12. End the session with distribution of the Self-Examination, Reflection, and Action Planning Handout. Suggest that the information on this handout will help participants implement what they learned today in their conflict management challenges back on the job. Give them a few minutes to study

the handout. Then ask for a show of hands indicating how many in the group can think of at least one potential conflict situation in their immediate future. Suggest that this handout can help them begin to plan for this very special kind of problem solving. Encourage them to start using this handout now, and resolve to continue with "First Feelings, Second Thoughts" as they return to work. Note that this handout has two sides.

REFERENCE

Goleman, D. (1995). *Emotional intelligence.* New York: Bantam Books.

HANDOUT 15.1

DISCUSSION STARTER HANDOUT FOR

Conflict Management

. . . .

"First Feelings, . . .

Fear

Dread

Fright

Anxiety

Suspicion

Confusion

A. A Ladder of Emotions

or

. . . Second Thoughts"

B. Think Win-Win

Source of quote: Emotional Intelligence, by Daniel Goleman. New York: Bantam Books, 1995.

HANDOUT 15.2

SELF-EXAMINATION, REFLECTION, AND ACTION PLANNING HANDOUT FOR
Conflict Management

. . . .

Self-Examination and Reflection

Reflect on your own personal strengths for coping with conflict. Look inward to assess your emotional intelligence and your cognitive ability to weigh alternatives, make decisions, and go above and beyond compromise.

Action Planning

Beginning now, write down at least three things that you can do to become a conflict manager, either on a personal level or at an organizational level.

1.

2.

3.

Then identify at least one situation that affects you at work, and design the beginnings of a plan to manage that situation's potential conflict before it escalates.

Conflict situation:

Emotional characteristics:

Cognitive characteristics:

16
· · · · · · · ·

Creativity

· ·

Can you think outside the box?

● PURPOSE

A creative workforce contributes to a company's longevity. Creativity in the everyday tasks of ordinary people doing their jobs is a traditional value and goal, especially in knowledge-based economies that are sweeping the globe. The purpose of this session is to explore the nature of creativity through participation in and study of several examples.

● SUMMARY

Companies that have encouraged creativity have risen to the top of economic and cultural life. But we are in danger of losing this important workplace value and goal, as work that demands creative thinking dissipates on its global journey. In this activity, participants will examine the nature of work-related creativity and define ways in which this workplace can encourage it.

● AGENDA

Step	Time
Discuss the example in the Discussion Starter Handout	5 minutes
Do the creativity exercise	15 minutes
Provide examples from the workplace	15 minutes
Describe current and desired practices in this workplace	10 minutes
Wrap up	10 minutes

● PREPARATION

Prior to the activity, copy the nine dots shown below onto a flip chart, but only use half the sheet vertically, allowing space for the solution, which you'll add later. Keep the sheet covered for showing later.

```
  •   •   •

  •   •   •

  •   •   •
```

The 9 Dots

● INTRODUCTION

1. As participants enter the room, distribute copies of the Discussion Starter Handout and ask them to study it.

2. Begin the session by introducing the topic and why it's important:

   "We're here today to talk about creativity. Some say that the United States' creative edge is disappearing; others say that the U.S. culture and economy will always encourage creative individuals. History shows that businesses that have fostered creativity and innovation have been highly successful from a profit point of view as well as a community contribution point of view. Creative workers are typically good problem solvers who enjoy a special kind of empowerment. Companies that facilitate creativity are known as good places to work.

"The handout you've received contains an example of a creative individual approaching his work, in this case the work of architecture. The wave-like curves and tilted angles of architect Frank Gehry's Guggenheim Museum in Bilbao, Spain, break with tradition of the 'white cube' concept used by most museum architects before Gehry. His approach to his work breaks patterns of line and shape, space and surface to produce what has been called an economic and cultural boon to the region on the banks of the Nervion River where the building stands. The five bullet points on the handout suggest some of the creative dimensions of Gehry's work. Take a look again at these five points."

● AWARENESS

3. After allowing 1 or 2 minutes for everyone to study the lines and the words in the handout, lead a discussion about the kinds of creativity shown in the Gehry example.

   Refer participants to the words in the Discussion Starter Handout. Ask them to pick out the key words that are descriptors for creativity. Get them started by saying, for example, "original," "risk taking," and so on. Record their comments on a flip chart.

4. Now show the "9 Dots" creativity exercise that you previously prepared on the flip chart. Ask the group to focus on the words from the Discussion Starter, "fresh approach," and the idea of thinking beyond "standards," beyond the establishment way of doing things. Explain that the task here is to draw four straight lines through these nine dots without retracing any lines and without lifting your pencil from the paper. Suggest that participants draw the nine dots on a piece of paper at their seats and try to do the exercise.

5. As people begin to work at the exercise, ask for a volunteer to come to the "9 Dots" on the flip chart and do the exercise in front of the group. Reiterate that they should listen carefully to the instructions; repeat them for the group:

   Draw four straight lines through these nine dots without retracing any lines and without lifting your pencil from the paper.

6. Remind them to think of Frank Gehry's dimensions of creativity and to follow his lead in "out of the cube" thinking. Expect some people to have done this exercise before and to remember how to do it. Others will experiment in various ways. Watch the group for apparent successes with the exercise, and after a few minutes ask for a show of hands indicating who "got it."

If the person at the flip chart still has not figured out the solution, ask one of these persons to help out at the flip chart.

7. If the volunteer at the flip chart has correctly solved the puzzle, show and explain it to the group. If the volunteer couldn't solve the puzzle, draw another set of nine dots and the solution as shown below.

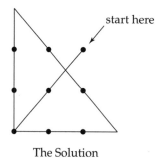

start here

The Solution

8. With this awareness of creativity from having experienced it, lead the group forward now to examination of workplace examples of creative thinking and of organizational supports for it.

● EXAMPLES

9. Transition into an examination of creativity in the workplace by asking the question of the group, "What is the creative turning point in the '9 Dots' exercise?"

Encourage participants, especially those who found the solution on their own, to say something like, "It had something to do with breaking the assumption of having to stay within the square box defined by the nine dots" or "It came when I literally started to think outside the box defined by the nine dots." Help them to realize that breaking assumptions is an important process in creative thinking—just like Frank Gehry thought and worked "outside the cube" of traditional museum architecture with his museum in Bilbao.

10. Ask the group whether they can point out some recent creative thinking on the part of manufacturing companies. Ask them to focus on consumer products

that broke the mold of traditional standards. Help them start finding current examples by suggesting that Crest Whitestrips™ is one. In this case, traditional toothpaste in a tube was the "broken" assumption—call it "thinking outside the tube." Another example might be the sterilized paper boxes of fruit juice produced by Motts™, Minute Maid™, and others. Known as "aseptic packaging," it's a different kind of sterilization process from the traditional glass jars or tin cans. It could be called "thinking outside the jar." Ask participants whether they can think of any other examples from the products they use. Focus on the creative risk taking of "breaking" assumptions. Keep discussion going for about 10 minutes.

● DEFINITION

11. As you move into discussion about this workplace, ask participants whether they can name any examples of creativity here. Introduce the term "intellectual capital," suggesting that brain power is worth a lot to a company, especially brain power that stays with a company and brain power that is capable of and encouraged to be creative. As the examples above show, both products and processes are worth examining in order to break old assumptions and challenge traditions. Use a flip chart to record participants' comments about this workplace. Do this yourself, or ask for a volunteer to act as scribe.

12. Now ask them to describe some of the innovative thinking processes required by any of these defined examples from this company. Ask them to think in terms of short phrases or single words such as:

   • Connect

   • Dig

   • Guess

   • Ask

   • Hypothesize

   • Restate

   • Reverse

   • Observe

   Ask participants to elaborate on their words, tying the words to what's happening in their organizations or what they see as creative directions in the company as a whole.

13. Finally, lead the group in discussion about their ideas on how the company can take action to support them individually or organizationally in their creative efforts. Suggest that organizations have many ways to define and support creativity and innovation. Use these questions to stir up their thinking. Ask for a show of hands after you read each question.

   • How many think that this company demonstrates that they value better performance, not just performance that meets standards?

   • How many think that this company helps creative ideas to surface beyond "business as usual"?

   • How many believe that the company "looks down on" learning from mistakes?

   • How many believe that their organization provides a working environment that encourages experimentation and examination?

   • How many have experienced ways to leverage creativity to meet business requirements?

   • How many have benefited from company-provided funds, personnel, and material resources to turn creative ideas into new products and services? Which products and services?

14. Close the thinking about how creativity is defined at this company by suggesting that participants' work on improving creativity will now begin as they return to their jobs.

● WRAP UP

15. To wrap up the session, reiterate the important benefits of workplace creativity: remaining competitive as a business, staying employed in work where you can make a contribution, better use of materials, more effective personnel practices, more interest from the community, more learning, more joy on the job. Ask the group if they can add any more benefits to themselves personally or to the company.

16. Distribute a copy of the Self-Examination, Reflection, and Action Planning Handout to each participant and suggest that they use this as a worksheet to improve creative thinking at this company. Note that it is two pages.

DISCUSSION STARTER HANDOUT FOR
Creativity

· ·

Some dimensions of architectural creativity:

- *Original thinking*
- *Fresh approach to architectural problems*
- *Ingenuity in construction and use of materials*
- *Positive risk taking regarding standards of the establishment*
- *Intuition in meeting demands of social purpose and visual excitement*

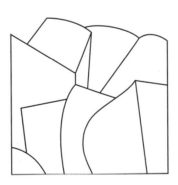

Guggenheim Museum, Bilbao, Spain
(Architect: Frank Gehry)

HANDOUT 16.2
SELF-EXAMINATION, REFLECTION, AND ACTION PLANNING HANDOUT FOR
Creativity

• •

Self-Examination

Turn inward to your own strengths and weaknesses, your competencies and needs regarding creativity. Challenge yourself to think about your responsibilities as an individual learner and as a team learner and to think about your own personal potential in this company.

Reflection

Focus on your own organization and name at least three things that the organization does now to encourage and support creativity and innovation. Ask yourself whether you are taking advantage of the opportunities here to be creative in your work.

1.

2.

3.

Action Planning

Renew your sense of mission for creative thinking and actions that can lead to innovation. Write yourself a memo of personal resolve to be more creative, using the format below. Include in the memo the development of several specific skills or competencies, name projects to which those skills and competencies can be applied, and suggest what effects and benefits your renewed efforts can be expected to have.

Memo

Date:

To: Myself

Re: Creative Resolve

17
. . . .

Self-Directed Learning
. . . .
Need to know versus nice to know

● PURPOSE

Being skilled at self-directed learning helps workers save time, become more productive, and contribute more intelligence to the business. The purpose of this session is to take a critical look at learners and learning in order to enable and empower participants to pursue the learning they need.

● SUMMARY

Becoming a self-directed learner is an increasingly critical goal for every worker. The pressures of time, productivity, and profit work together to demand more individualized learning more relevant to specific jobs—need to know rather than nice to know. In this activity, participants will examine what it means to be a self-directed learner and will contrast this with traditional training. Participants will examine their own experiences as learners and discuss examples of the best parts of various kinds of workplace learning.

● AGENDA

Step	Time
Discuss the Discussion Starter Handout	15 minutes
Provide examples from the workplace	15 minutes
Describe current and desired practices in the workplace	10 minutes
Wrap up	10 minutes

● INTRODUCTION

1. As participants enter the room, distribute copies of the Discussion Starter Handout and ask them to read it.

2. Begin the session by introducing the topic and why it's important:

> "We're here today to talk about self-directed learning. Business pressures are driving the transition from trainer-designed and instructor-led learning opportunities to self-directed learning from work itself. The challenges to individuals to become more skilled and more knowledgeable on their own as their work demands it are being driven by time, productivity, and profit.

> "The Asian proverb on the Discussion Starter Handout talks about 'eating for a lifetime.' It is a metaphor for 'learning for a lifetime.' When we have learned to fish by ourselves, our hunger can be satisfied; when we have learned to learn by ourselves, our curiosity, creativity, and productivity can be satisfied. In this session, we will examine the personal motivations to become a self-directed learner as well as examine some of the tools an individual self-directed learner can use to adopt a life-long learning habit. Think: 'I need to eat, so I will learn to fish.'"

● AWARENESS

3. Ask participants to look at the handout. Suggest that they imagine themselves at the end of that fishing pole. Help participants to focus their thinking on being the initiator of action, like being the fisherman.

4. Turn their attention to the essential difference between having training presented to them versus learning directed by them. Refer again to the handout and suggest that "Learning to fish in order to eat for a lifetime" is like learning to be a self-directed learner in order to learn for a lifetime. Discovering where the fish are every day and catching them yourself is very different from having the fish presented to you on your plate. Practically speaking, self-directed learning begins with an acceptance on the part of the worker of his or her role as the one responsible for learning—not the instructional designer or the instructor or the media whiz with elaborate show-and-tell programs on state-of-the-art projectors. Ask for a show of hands on the following questions to illustrate the differences in approach to learning:

   • How many of you have attended training sessions that were off-target to what you needed for your job?

   • How many of you were asked by management to go to a training session that had no relevance to the gaps in your performance?

   • How many of you have taken training in your own hands and simply asked a fellow worker to explain something to you or show you how to do something related to your job?

   • How many of you have a pretty good idea what you need to know to do a good job?

   • What percentage of training would you say is a waste of time and money? 50%? 35%? 10%? Other percent?

5. Help participants to think about today's challenges and motivations for being self-directed learners by asking the following questions:

   • Do you believe that work is personally satisfying?

   • Do you believe that learning is an opportunity for growth?

   • Do you believe in your own ability to learn?

   • Do you know what you need to know and do in order to work smarter?

   • Can you see possibilities for learning new knowledge and skills from the work that you currently are responsible for?

   • Do you like to learn at your own pace?

   • Can you define your own personal learning style?

   • Do you sometimes resent the time you spend away from your job when you go to seminars or classroom training?

6. Lead a discussion about participants' beliefs and motivations about self-directed learning. Reinforce any comments they make that indicate their readiness to take control of their learning and become self-directed learners.

● EXAMPLES

7. Tell participants that for approximately the next 15 minutes they'll be asked to name some successful traditional classroom training in this company's classrooms or off-site, as well as identify some opportunities for learning from work itself on the job. Label two flip-chart pages, side by side, one "Traditional Training" and the other "Self-Directed Learning." Ask for a volunteer scribe to record their responses as you continue to focus on facilitation of discussion.

● DEFINITION

8. Introduce the concept of "blended learning," defined as a combination of traditional and self-directed learning. Bring in the concept of e-learning or using the Internet and Web to support learning and the possibilities of learning with the support and involvement of coaches or mentors. Suggest that there's a support role for the company in providing opportunities for learning at work from work. Ask the group what they see as the company's role in providing learning opportunities for them and how they think this company is doing. Facilitate discussion and use the flip chart to record ideas. Be prepared to include some kinds of classroom instruction whose success depends on face-to-face interaction. Engage in discussion about the positive features and effects of all kinds of learning systems and situations—classroom, e-learning, coaching, self-directed.

● WRAP UP

9. To close the session, focus only on the self-directed learner and some of the key requirements for self-directed learning to be successful. Ask participants to give you their ideas, either based on experience or on what they would like to do. Use a flip chart to record their ideas.

10. Start by suggesting a few of the following items; supplement their list with any of these they haven't thought of. Self-directed learners need to:

- Identify their own personal preferences about when and where to learn

- Identify and describe their own needs for information and skills

- Describe their own individual learning style (for example, one who likes rules, or one who likes to get warm feelings while learning, or one who always jumps to the applications of what was learned, or one who likes to experiment, one who likes to sit and think for a while, one who needs to talk it over with a buddy, and so on)

- Identify the resources they'll need to solve their learning problems

- Figure out where to find the resources and estimate the cost in time and money

- Describe a self-monitoring system and set standards for evaluation

- Create a learning plan, with objectives and milestone dates

- Establish a knowledge network of content resources and helpful people

- Expect failure, correct it, and learn from it

- Document success

- Share new skills and knowledge with others who can benefit from this knowledge and its applications

- Be first a learner, then a teacher

11. Distribute a copy of the two-page Self-Examination, Reflection, and Action Planning Handout to each participant and explain that participants can use this worksheet to help organize their thoughts. Challenge participants to be assertive in their search for learning opportunities in their work.

12. Suggest that participants talk over with their supervisors or team members any ideas they have for increasing their effectiveness as self-directed learners.

DISCUSSION STARTER HANDOUT FOR
Self-Directed Learning

"Give me a fish and I eat for a day;

Teach me to fish and I eat for a lifetime."

Asian proverb

HANDOUT 17.2

SELF-EXAMINATION, REFLECTION, AND ACTION PLANNING HANDOUT FOR
Self-Directed Learning

• •

Self-Examination

Self-directed learning is promoted as not only a way to maximize resources and realize economies, but also a way to empower individuals to seek learning opportunities whenever and wherever they can be found. System change is complemented by psychological challenge to individuals to learn as they need to learn according to their own learning styles and choices of supports and tools for learning.

Return to the Asian proverb of the Discussion Starter Handout and review the challenge of "learning to fish." Think about your own roles as a responsible and empowered employee. Use this as a checklist for refocusing your thinking as a self-directed learner.

As a self-directed learner, I need to:

- Identify my own personal preferences about when and where to learn

- Identify and describe my own needs for information and skills

- Describe my own individual learning style (for example, one who likes rules, or one who likes to get warm feelings while learning, or one who always jumps to the applications of what was learned, or one who likes to experiment, one who likes to sit and think for a while, one who needs to talk it over with a buddy, and so on)

- Identify the resources I'll need to solve my learning problems

- Figure out where to find resources and estimate the cost in time and money

- Describe a self-monitoring system and set standards for evaluation

- Create a learning plan, with objectives and milestone dates

- Establish a knowledge network of content resources and helpful people

- Expect failure, correct it, and learn from it

- Document success

- Share the new knowledge and its applications with others who can benefit from this knowledge and applications

- Be first a learner, then a teacher

Reflection

Working smarter has been the challenge to American workers for at least a decade. The U.S. Department of Labor periodically releases information about the skills knowledge workers need, periodically suggesting that "workers can't think" and that companies need to do something about this. As you reflect on your motivations and competencies for self-directed learning, think about how you can contribute to your company's success through on-the-job, self-directed learning.

Action Planning

Choose three areas of personal development as a self-directed learner for your own growth and for the growth of the business. Write down these three things and return to your job with renewed responsibility and motivation.

1.

2.

3.

18
• • • • • • •

Time Management

• •

What? Why? When? Where? Who?

● PURPOSE

Managing one's time at work is a foundation for effective relationships and high performance. The purpose of this session is to develop skills and strategies to manage time wisely for the sake of accountability, productivity, and a healthier and more enjoyable work life.

● SUMMARY

In today's fast-paced and demanding workplace, it is critical that individuals develop skills and understanding to deal with the pressures of time. Teamwork and flatter organizations push time management down to the individual worker level, making it even more important for individuals to develop the strategies and skills to manage themselves. In this session, participants will discuss a variety of time management techniques and principles in order to assess their needs for help in managing their own time. Action planning will follow the session.

● AGENDA

Step	Time
Discuss examples in the Discussion Starter Handout	10 minutes
Provide examples from the workplace	20 minutes
Describe current individual techniques in use	15 minutes
Wrap up	10 minutes

● PREPARATION

Prior to the session, prepare a flip chart with the words shown in Step 6.

● INTRODUCTION

1. As participants enter the room, distribute copies of the Discussion Starter Handout and ask them to read it.

2. Begin the session by introducing the topic and why it's important:

> "We're here today to talk about individual time management strategies and skills. Organizational life has changed in the last few years: teamwork and flatter organizations push time management down to the individual worker level; and computers, e-mail, and Internet technologies make demands on our time to do things faster, better, and in greater quantity. Accountability systems hang over us like never before. The real frontier in time management is in the job of the ordinary employee. This session will help you define what needs to be done and why, and will focus on the skills you need to make your own work life more enjoyable and productive through time management.

> "The handout you received has examples of what two national seminar providers are saying in their advertisements in order to connect with the needs of a broad base of workers. If you've not done so already, please read the examples now."

3. Allow about 1 minute for participants to read the Discussion Starter Handout. Then ask them to pick out the words that signal the most frustrating pressures. Keep discussion going for about 5 minutes to let participants "vent" a little in order to get an idea of what the pressing time management problems seem to be in their organizations.

4. After all participants seem to have had their say, draw their attention to the last question on the Discussion Starter Handout, namely, "Are you doing more and enjoying it less?" Ask for a show of hands: How many say yes? How many say no? Then ask the yes voters what some of the other pressures on their time are, referring still to the handout. To help them start, say the words "Quicker results?" or "Seduced by a hundred e-mails?" Raise the awareness level about the demands on their time.

5. If anyone says no, they are not doing more and are not enjoying it less, and things seem to be okay, ask those folks to describe for the group what strategies or techniques they're using to cope with the demands of managing their time. Use any positive comments and tips to make a transition into the next activity.

6. Show the prepared flip chart with the following words:

faster	immediate	start	end	plan
increase	decrease	document	remember	urgent
eliminate	combine	focus	leverage	ASAP

You'll use these to stimulate participants' ideas about specific strategies for time management.

7. Ask participants to use these words to connect with their own experiences on the job. Ask them to choose two or three words that have had an impact on their success or failure at time management. Call on individuals to share their stories, and facilitate a discussion around their chosen words. Ask them whether they'd like to add any key words to the list.

● EXAMPLES

8. Tell the group that for approximately the next 20 minutes, they'll be talking about specific good ideas they can adopt—good ideas that have worked for others who made a commitment to better time management. Use the following list as a guide:

   1. Analyze practices to see whether steps can be eliminated (for example, management signoffs, unnecessary documentation, group meetings, and so on).

   2. Batch or chunk related activities to maximize the momentum in dealing with them.

   3. Start and end meetings on time; don't accommodate those who wander in late by taking time away from those who came when they were supposed to come.

   4. Do better analysis of individual needs for training; pay attention to learning styles.

   5. Provide on-the-job coaches, online performance support, clear performance standards.

   6. Handle paper only once; address its contents and don't put it on "the pile" for later.

   7. Prioritize; do the first things first and the right things right.

   8. Be disciplined about e-mail; figure out a system that works for you and stick to it.

   9. Don't let people who interrupt you get comfortable either in your office or on the phone.

   10. Know where your time goes; keep an honest record for two weeks; make changes according to the facts you've assembled.

   11. Understand the work systems in which you operate; shorten tasks, know what and who is related or integral to your job performance and figure out how to make more efficient interfaces; identify critical paths of processes.

12. Come prepared to meetings and training events; know what the objectives are, not only the agendas, and be sure that those objectives are your objectives. If meetings and training events don't fit with your objectives, don't go.

9. For each item, ask: "How many of you have found this technique useful in your job?" Make a list of numbers 1 through 12, recording the frequency count next to each as appropriate. Ask for a volunteer scribe to keep a tally on the flip chart, like this: 1. / / / / 2. / / 3. / / / / /, and so on. Then go back to the numbers that have the most interesting tallies for one reason or another and talk about them.

● DEFINITION

10. Now tell participants that the next task in this session is to work toward a definition of this company's main issues in time management. Use the recorded frequency counts on the flip chart for ideas, asking the group to define the main issues based on what today's discussion has been. Create a definition of time management at this company. Focus on the company as a whole; later they'll focus on their own personal techniques for improvement. Do this as a bullet list or a narrative statement at the flip chart. Do this as a group exercise, accepting ideas that are different from your own. Remind participants to make their own contributions to the definition and to withhold judgment about others' ideas that differ from their own ideas. Aim for a list or narrative containing at least five issues.

11. Before leaving the topic of definition, address the issues just recorded, one by one. Talk about one or more specific techniques or strategies that individual employees could use to solve time management problems expressed in these issues.

● WRAP UP

12. To close the session, make a statement to the effect that the workplace has changed in response to the pressures of time and is not likely to go back to a slower-paced era. Reiterate that it is critical for individuals to develop skills and strategies to manage their time wisely for the sake of accountability, productivity, relationships with colleagues, and a healthier and more enjoyable work life.

13. Challenge participants to return to the job ready to reflect on the time management issues in this workplace that directly affect them and to resolve to take individual actions to address the issues.

14. Distribute a copy of the two-page Self-Examination, Reflection, and Action Planning Handout to each participant and explain to them that they can use this as a worksheet as they organize their thoughts and actions.

HANDOUT 18.1
DISCUSSION STARTER HANDOUT FOR
Time Management

· ·

. . . seen in ads for seminars . . .

Faster ideas

Immediate use

Quicker results

Shorter time

GoInnovateAcademy

Is urgency always valid?

*Are you seduced by the hundred
e-mails waiting for you?*

Wasn't the computer supposed to eliminate paper?

Are you doing more and enjoying it less?

American Management Association Seminar 2233

HANDOUT 18.2

SELF-EXAMINATION, REFLECTION, AND ACTION PLANNING HANDOUT FOR

Time Management

. . . .

Self-Examination

Every employee needs actionable ideas for time management, especially given today's electronically networked environment, the employee empowerment movement, and flatter organizations. Take some time to examine where you fit in this workplace picture; make a clear and simple statement of your own personal needs for better time management practices.

Reflection

Reflect on the following statements: "My time is my responsibility, and my goal as an employee is to work smarter" and "I will not waste my time, nor waste the time of other employees with whom I interact."

Action Planning

Take the challenge to improve your individual performance through a personal plan for better time-management behaviors. Jot down five specific actions you can take to become a better time manager. Share some of these actions with others who might be impacted by what you do.

1.

2.

3.

4.

5.

19

. . . .

Valuing Differences

. . . .

We're all in this thing together!

● PURPOSE

For companies to reap the benefits of a diverse workforce, they first must help workers to value differences. The purpose of this session is to analyze a mini-case study in valuing differences and, by identifying problems and solutions in it, become more able to identify problems and work toward solutions in this workplace.

● SUMMARY

An increasingly important topic for all workers is that of valuing differences. When diversity issues arise in the workplace, it is critical that individuals have a process in place to first identify problems and then to work on solutions. Fundamental to effective management of workplace diversity is the corporate supports that are in place to indicate and demonstrate that this company values differences. In this activity, participants will analyze a mini-case study that contains some problems in valuing differences. The group will identify the problems and suggest solutions that the company or the key players in the mini-case study could implement. After discussion of the mini-case study, participants will turn their attention to this workplace and identify examples of problems and solutions here.

● AGENDA

Step	Time
Discuss the mini-case study in the Discussion Starter Handout	20 minutes
Provide examples from the workplace	15 minutes
Describe current and desired practices in the workplace	15 minutes
Wrap up	5 minutes

● INTRODUCTION

1. As participants enter the room, distribute copies of the Discussion Starter Handout and ask them to read it, paying particular attention to the question at the bottom of the page. Suggest that as they read the mini-case study, they try to identify the problems that the story of Lludek and Stacey raises. Suggest that they make notes in the margins to guide later discussions.

2. Begin the session by introducing the topic and why it's important:

> "We hear a great deal about managing diversity in our workplaces. Federal, state, and local laws and corporate guidelines are part of our standards for behavior in schools and workplaces. Companies like to publicize the successes they've had in managing diversity; organizations, teams, managers, and mentors all develop ways of being more inclusive and aware.

> "This session, however, focuses on what comes before the management of diversity, and this is how we 'value differences' in the workplace. Valuing differences involves the emotional or affective skills we need to develop before we can follow the laws and rules of managing diversity. In valuing differences, think of support systems and personal relationships. When individuals know how to value differences and act accordingly, the job of managing diversity becomes much easier.

> "The handout you've received contains a mini-case study from an actual company. Refer back to it now and review its key problems and your notes in the margin."

3. Allow at least 5 minutes for participants to read the mini-case study of Lludek and Stacey and to think about the identification of problems separately from the suggestion of solutions. Ask them to focus first on identification of the problems.

4. Then facilitate a discussion about the problems they can identify. Suggest that they begin by identifying the differences between Lludek and Stacey. Use a flip chart to record their responses or ask for a volunteer to act as scribe for this activity.

5. Next, ask participants to identify the problems in the corporate environment that are explicitly stated in the mini-case study or are implied "between the lines." Record these on the flip chart too. Post the flip-chart pages side by side.

6. Suggest that the skills needed to value differences are often found in the emotional characteristics and competencies of workers. That is, valuing differences is not just a matter of following rules and abiding by laws. Ask participants to suggest what some of these emotional skills might be that would have made the Lludek/Stacey encounter more productive. Get them started by suggesting any of these:

   - patience
   - awareness of cultural patterns
   - tolerance of cultural patterns
   - desire to improve
   - self-awareness

   - self-control
   - empathy
   - motivation
   - influencing
   - overcoming stereotypes

7. Now direct their attention to the question at the bottom of the Discussion Starter Handout: "What could this R&D company have done in terms of valuing differences to make Lludek and Stacey's encounter more effective and productive?" Engage the group in discussion about the mini-case study. Ask for their constructive criticism of the individuals and the company involved in this brief encounter. Seek answers to the question, focusing on how the company in the mini-case study could have helped these two employees to value their differences. It is this framework of both individual and organizational competencies through which we look at the issues in the Lludek/Stacey encounter.

Talk about the behaviors of each of the characters, Lludek and Stacey, and about the organizational resources and supports, or lack thereof, for the workshop development task they have been assigned. Focus on the differences that are apparent or suggested in the mini-case study, and by extension on the problems that not valuing these differences in an intentional way seems to have caused. Discuss differences in language, age, gender, ethnicity, professional focus, personal style, negotiation ability, work environment, knowledge or skill development, emotional state, and so on.

● EXAMPLES

8. Now turn the discussion to this workplace and the issues involved in valuing differences here. Remind the group that problem identification comes before solution identification. As a way to move the group from the mini-case study to the reality of their workplace, ask participants whether they know what categories are mentioned in this company's non-discrimination statement. Use a flip chart to record their responses. Typical ones are listed below. Wait until all of these have been said (or bring them up yourself if necessary) before continuing.

   • Race

   • Age

   • Gender

   • Religion

   • Sexual orientation

   • Disability

   • National origin

9. Explain that the list above is the typical guideline a company has for managing diversity. That is, this list is the government-mandated anti-discrimination benchmark. Suggest to them that there is also another list, one of secondary categories that often hinder an individual's, team's, or company's abilities to value differences. These secondary categories, some of which were evidenced in the mini-case study, are often the ones that require our deeper analysis in

order to be able to truly demonstrate that we value differences. Present the following list; ask the group to add any other categories they can think of from this company or society at large:

- Education level

- Class

- Neighborhood

- Dress

- Income/buying power

- Intelligence

- Employment position/level

- Computer savvy

- Language competence

● DEFINITION

10. As participants focus on this company, ask them to describe the positive things they observe or have experienced regarding valuing differences. For example, someone might say, "I think it's good how teams are put together with age, gender, race, and position level represented" or "I think it's a good idea to require the special 'valuing differences' training for all employees" or "It's good to see a variety of people eating together in the cafeteria" or "I'm glad we have an LGTB (Lesbian, Gay, Transgender, Bisexual) Club here and that the company funds their programs." Keep the discussion general; that is, do not probe deeply into personal issues or embarrass anyone.

11. Conclude this definition activity by asking participants to define some additional programs, relationships, or communications that they'd like to see started at this company in order to increase employees' abilities to value differences. Record these on a flip chart yourself or ask for a volunteer scribe to do so.

● WRAP UP

12. To close, review three key concepts from this session:

    • Valuing differences is a foundation for effective management of diversity.

    • Being able to value differences requires various kinds of emotional strength.

    • Companies have a responsibility to provide a supportive environment so that employees can grow in understanding and competence in valuing differences.

13. Distribute a copy of the Self-Examination, Reflection, and Action Planning Handout to each participant and explain that participants can use this worksheet to plan their greater understanding of and participation in valuing differences in this company.

HANDOUT 19.1
DISCUSSION STARTER HANDOUT FOR
Valuing Differences

● ●

Mini-Case Study of Lludek and Stacey

Lludek is an exceptionally brilliant software engineer recently assigned to a prestigious project at a famous R&D laboratory. He is Polish and has a poor command of English, particularly written English. He is forty-six years old.

Stacey is a typical fresh-faced American trainer, physically attractive and always overtly friendly. She is a behind-the-scenes member of the course development team at the lab and has been assigned to help Lludek write up his project as a workshop that can be attended by interested persons throughout the company. Stacey is twenty-six years old. Both Lludek and Stacey have doctorate degrees in their professional fields.

They agree on a time for a first meeting to get started with the workshop design and locate a small empty office in which to meet. The office is about 8 feet by 8 feet and is furnished with an old steel desk, a desk chair, an empty bookcase, and an extra chair by the bookcase. It has a fluorescent light that only half works, and the office has one small window overlooking the parking lot and dumpsters.

Lludek has arrived in the office first and is standing behind the desk chair near the window. Stacey bounces in, closes the door, and puts her notebooks down on the desk and quickly gets down to business, talking animatedly about objectives, evaluations, slides, handouts, and other course development jargon.

Lludek grabs the back of the desk chair and moves with great agitation from side to side behind the desk, frequently glancing out the window. Stacey moves in and partially sits on a corner of the desk, in order to get closer to him in hopes that they can at least make eye contact and get on with their assignment.

After some preliminary attempts at connecting ideas, they both agree to set another date and try again.

The question is:
What could this R&D company have done in terms of valuing differences to make Lludek and Stacey's encounter more effective and productive?

Lunch and Learn. Copyright © 2006 by John Wiley & Sons, Inc. Reproduced by permission of Pfeiffer, an Imprint of Wiley. www.pfeiffer.com

---

SELF-EXAMINATION, REFLECTION, AND ACTION PLANNING HANDOUT FOR
Valuing Differences

• •

Self-Examination and Reflection

Now turn inward for self-examination regarding the examples you discussed in the group session. Identify your own place as a contributor to one or more of the problems and resolve to take action in your own way to develop solutions. Reflect on your stereotypes and prejudices; separate values, beliefs, opinions, and facts. Document your self-analysis on a simple chart for your own reference only. Following is a sample format:

Scale: 1–7

1 = low contribution to this problem	7 = high contribution to this problem
List of Problems in Valuing Differences	My Scale Rating

Action Planning

Create an action plan for yourself that includes both kinds of corrective actions: those that you personally can take to improve your own ability at valuing differences, and those that you can take at an organizational level to improve the capacity of the company to value differences. Give yourself timelines, standards, monitoring techniques, and markers for success.

Teams

20

....

Alignment

....

Together we'll go far

● PURPOSE

In this activity, participants will tackle the issue of "alignment," best described as getting the team working together—important for efficient and effective teamwork. The purpose of this session is to increase participant awareness of processes that lead to efficiency and effectiveness of teamwork.

● SUMMARY

Participants, working at a flip chart, will consider how various elements of their team or organization are either aligned with or counter to the overall organizational direction.

● AGENDA

Step	Time
Discuss all of the arrows in the Discussion Starter Handout	15 minutes
Provide examples from the workplace	10 minutes
Do the flip-chart activity defining current practices in this workplace	20 minutes
Wrap up	10 minutes

● PREPARATION

For the definition phase, you will need to have prepared two items ahead of the meeting time for this session. One of these is a drawing of a large arrow to be drawn on the flip chart, similar to the one in the Discussion Starter Handout, but without the smaller arrows in it. Use the whole diagonal length of a page of the flip chart. Participants will fill this in with their own alignment and integration issues.

Second, have several rectangular pads of small sticky notes available for participants to use. Prepare one sticky note as an example of what you want them to do as they define their team's alignment and integration situation. Take one sticky note off the pad, draw an arrow on it big enough to be filled in with two words, and stick it on the flip chart somewhere outside of the big arrow as an example for the group to use. Your preparation should look something like this:

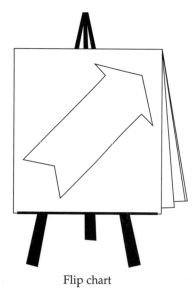

Flip chart

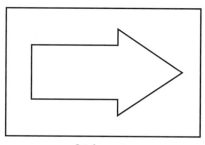

Sticky note

● INTRODUCTION

1. As participants enter the room, distribute copies of the Discussion Starter Handout and ask them to study it. Tell them that this will be a sample for an activity they'll do in a few minutes.

2. Begin the session by introducing the topic and why it's important:

   "We're here today to talk about alignment and its importance in build-ing and maintaining teams. Integration of personalities and moving in the same direction are tough parts of teamwork. It is often said that working in a team is contradictory to the United States' reputation for valuing individuals and entrepreneurship, but teams persist anyway and are found in most American workplaces. Teams that succeed are aligned teams, with the team's individuals clearly involved in processes that parallel the direction of the team.

   "Getting a team to work together involves studying all of the influences on the team from throughout the workplace and working to line them up with the major direction and mission of the team. The graphic repre-sentation of many small arrows within a big arrow is an appropriate representation of what's involved in working toward alignment. Think of the big arrow as the team.

   "The handout you received contains small arrows going in different directions within the big arrow. The task of alignment is to rotate those small arrows so that they go the same direction as the big arrow. Other small arrows could be added, of course, to reflect specific organizational realities and challenges. If you've not already done so, please study the handout now."

● AWARENESS

3. After allowing a few minutes for everyone to study the handout, lead a discussion about the obvious major alignment problems with this team represented by the graphic.

   Tell participants that they'll be referring to this handout for the next 10 min-utes or more. Suggest that they focus on the small arrow, customer value, as a place to start. Ask them to notice that this issue is going in exactly the opposite direction from the direction of the team as a whole. Policies and accountability are not far behind. This kind of analysis can be helpful in visualizing problem areas and beginning to figure out what needs to be done to bring specific things back into alignment.

4. Shift the discussion to the small arrows that are in alignment or nearly in alignment. Ask the group to identify them.

5. Suggest that this kind of alignment graphic could be used in another way, by using verbs instead of nouns. For example, the small arrows could be stated as:

- Abolish bureaucracy
- Quit cover-ups
- Stop lying
- Go beyond meeting standards
- Make decisions
- Find solutions

- Accept your mistakes
- Bury your ego
- Ignore status
- Share the good times
- Learn from failure
- Act on your convictions

And so on. Using action words is often a more potent way to describe a challenge.

● EXAMPLES

6. Challenge participants now to identify the teams at work in this company. Get them to begin to think in broader terms than identifying only their own team. If there are only a few teams in this company, list teams that participants think should be functioning at this company. Write the names of these teams on a flip chart as participants name them.

● DEFINITION

7. Now refer participants to the large arrow on the flip chart that you previously prepared.

8. Pass around several packs of small (1½ by 2 inches) sticky notes, instructing participants to take off three or four to use in the flip-chart activity coming up. Explain that each participant is expected to contribute two ideas. The extras

are in case mistakes are made. Ask the group to use a black medium-point marker, which you will now hand out. (Put the markers in water glasses or coffee mugs and pass them around the room.)

9. Tell the group that you'd like to have 100 percent participation in this definition activity. Direct them to focus on this company and on a specific team of which they are a member, or, if they are not team members, to continue the activity based on what they believe or have heard about teamwork.

10. The challenge to the group now is to ask participants to make two sticky notes each on which they will draw an empty arrow and write one alignment challenge. As they finish writing on the two sticky-note arrows that they have just drawn, ask them to get up and post their arrows on the big flip-chart arrow in whatever direction they believe is appropriate. Refer back to the dialogue starter as a sample.

11. When the big arrow is filled in, start the discussion about the participants' creation and what's on the flip chart. Note any repeat topics on the small arrows. Note any clear indications of positive and of negative issues and actions. Keep discussion going until the group is satisfied with the definition of team alignment at this company, but not for more than 20 minutes.

● WRAP UP

12. To close the session, acknowledge that the work of teams is hard work and that the analysis done here today at the flip chart with the sticky notes can provide some help.

13. Tell participants that as they leave this session, they should ask themselves:

   • At what point can I make a difference? or

   • What processes do I personally need to realign in order to be more effective as a team player?

   Challenge them to take some time for self-examination, reflection, and action planning as they go back to work.

14. Distribute a copy of the Self-Examination, Reflection, and Action Planning Handout to each participant and explain that participants can use this as a worksheet to help organize their thoughts. Note that it has two sides.

DISCUSSION STARTER HANDOUT FOR
Alignment

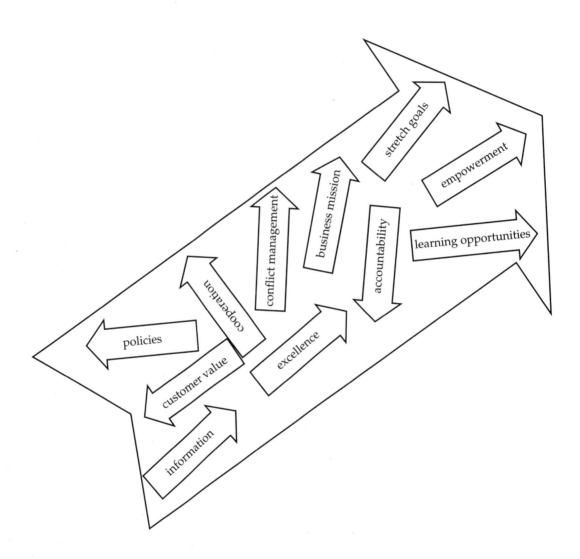

Source: Adapted from "Paralysis," in *More Team Games for Trainers* (pp. 27–30) by C. Nilson. New York: McGraw-Hill, 1998. Copyright © The McGraw-Hill Companies, Inc. Used with permission.

HANDOUT 20.2

SELF-EXAMINATION, REFLECTION, AND
ACTION PLANNING HANDOUT FOR
Alignment

• •

Self-Examination

Think for a few minutes about priorities; that is, recalling the flip-chart activity
and the Discussion Starter Handout, think about what needs to be done first,
second, third, and so on in this company to start things going in the right direction.
Identify things that you personally can do to help things line up.

Reflection

Reflect on the flip-chart activity in which participants in the *Lunch and Learn*
session placed small arrows in various directions. Think about what kinds of
individual action plans regarding team alignment should be created. Think
about how many alignment activities there are across the company in which you
personally can make a positive contribution. Identify several people, perhaps some
in the *Lunch and Learn* session, with whom you personally can collaborate to make
things better.

Action Planning

Narrow your planning to three priority actions you will take to better align team-work in this company, either with your own team or with another team described in the session. Specify dates and specific other persons who need to be involved with you.

Action	Who	When
•		
•		
•		
•		
•		

21
. . . .

Building a Team

Get them all on the same page!

● **PURPOSE**

Building a team has its own special requirements in order for the team to function effectively. The purpose of this session is to analyze the organizational factors in putting a team together.

● **SUMMARY**

In this activity, participants will analyze a mini-case study of team building in its earliest stage. The case study activity will provide examples of what to consider in forming any team. Participants will then focus on team building in their organizations and identify some of the special requirements for team building at this company.

● AGENDA

Step	Time
Discuss the mini-case study in the Discussion Starter Handout	15 minutes
Provide examples from the workplace	15 minutes
Describe current and desired practices in the workplace	15 minutes
Wrap up	10 minutes

● INTRODUCTION

1. As participants enter the room, distribute copies of the Discussion Starter Handout and ask them to read it. Allow about 3 minutes for this.

2. Begin the session by introducing the topic and why it's important:

> "We're here today to talk about building a team. We all know that a team is different from a group or a committee, but often we don't give too much thought to the special requirements of getting a team going. We'll set the stage for identifying and explaining those special requirements by analyzing a mini-case study. We'll then go on to talk about the requirements of teams in this company.

> "The handout you received is a case study of the very earliest stages of building a team, in this case, a senator's Constituent Awareness Team. If you've not done so already, please read the handout now. Pay attention to the major ideas and characteristics of the individuals in the mini-case."

● AWARENESS

3. After allowing about 3 to 5 minutes for participants to read and think about the mini-case of building the senator's team, lead a discussion about it. Help the group identify elements of thought and action required in forming the senator's team. The following questions can be used to help guide this discussion:

- What is the goal of this team (for example, to provide information to constituents)?

- What are some of the tasks the team is being asked to do (for example, design formats, find positive examples of the senator's work, contact constituents, and so on)?

- What will it take for this mix of people to get together as a team (for example, get to know each other better, identify and share information, leverage their individual work assignments into the team's goal, leadership from the senator, and so on)?

- What are some of the obstacles you see to building the senator's team (for example, different personalities, all new employees, work assignments in different areas from each other, having to get access to the right information, needing to know the variety of constituent interest throughout the state, team tasks taking up a lot of time away from regular job assignments, and others)?

4. Use the flip chart to list these key words:

- Goals

- People mix

- Access to information

- Organizational readiness

- Obstacles

Suggest that these could be considered the building blocks of forming a team. It's not enough to just want to form a team.

● EXAMPLES

5. Now turn participants' attention to the real world of teams they know. Ask them to identify several good examples of existing teams, either here in this company or in other organizations. Ask them to say why they think so and tell what they have observed that those teams do that makes them outstanding. Bring the group discussion back to team building, if it goes off track.

● DEFINITION

6. Next, tell participants that the group will come up with a definition of team-building ideas and techniques for this company. Ask for a show of hands in answer to the question: "Who in this room is a member of a team here?" This will help make the transition from consideration of "other" teams to consideration of teams at this company.

7. Ask the group to think back to when their own teams were formed, or to think about what they'd do now if they were in charge of building a team. Use the flip chart to record the group's analysis of ideas for building teams that would work—or do work—in this company. Write down all ideas, or ask for a volunteer from the group to act as scribe. Then circle key words among their comments on the flip chart or ask for a volunteer from the group to circle the key words. Refer to the list of key words (Step 4, written on the flip chart) from the mini-case study and compare and contrast both sets of key words—those from the senator's team versus the key words from participants' experience that the group has just identified and circled.

8. Try to get a good idea of which ideas or strategies in this company are the ones on which to focus when building a team here. Consider the reasons why certain things can or do work here and the reasons why certain things do not work here. Consider ideas for improving the early stages of team building in organizations at this company.

● WRAP UP

9. To close the session, restate the importance of the early stages of team building. Emphasize the analysis that has to precede the development of a team, and urge participants to resolve to do the right things right. Highlight the important key words from the flip charts.

10. Tell participants that the ideas of this *Lunch and Learn* session should continue back at their workplaces with self-examination, reflection, and action planning.

11. Before they return to their jobs and become involved in team building in one way or another, suggest that they ask themselves these questions:

- How can my job be strengthened by working in a team?

- What are my particular personality strengths that could be helpful in building a team?

- Is a team approach right for the goals I have for my work?

- Can I identify the resources we need in order to form a team?

- What are the obstacles to team building in this company, and can I help to overcome them for myself and for others?

- Can I explain the benefits of working in teams in my organization?

12. Distribute a copy of the Self-Examination, Reflection, and Action Planning Handout to each participant and explain that participants can use this as a worksheet to help organize their thoughts.

13. (*optional*) Suggest that like-minded participants get together over the next week or two to talk about and begin planning for team building in this company and carry through on their individual action planning.

HANDOUT 21.1
DISCUSSION STARTER HANDOUT FOR
Building a Team

• •

Mini-Case Study: The Senator's Team

Doug, Anna, Eric, and Peter were first-year associates in the Washington, D.C., office of a senator from Eric's state. The senator saw an opportunity for forming a team with the nucleus of these four new employees, all recent graduates with master's degrees in government or American history. He called the four associates together and announced that they would be known as the "Constituent Awareness Team," whose team goal it would be to design and provide information to constituents in his home state about the good things that were happening around the D.C. office.

These four individuals were drinking buddies but not particularly friends. Doug and Anna had just celebrated their marriage and come back from their honeymoon, Eric was always happy to take a quick weekend trip to Atlantic City or Foxwoods casinos, and Peter was a cerebral type who still read history books and went to museums in his spare time. Their work assignments varied from meeting and greeting visitors, taking minutes at staff meetings, studying the *Congressional Record* for items of interest to the senator, to Labor Department research with an impact on the senator's home state.

SELF-EXAMINATION, REFLECTION, AND ACTION PLANNING HANDOUT FOR
Building a Team

. . . .

Self-Examination

Take some time to identify your ideas, your self-revelations, and your intuitions on action steps about the examples you identified in the *Lunch and Learn* session. If you discover that your own thinking has been limited by lack of information or lack of awareness and that ideas put forth by others in the group are worth your adopting, tell them about your leap of learning and thank others for their insight and wisdom. Connecting on many different levels is a good beginning to good teamwork.

Reflection

Reflect in a synthesizing way about the discussions. Consider points of view, learning styles, personality differences, and, above all, your own perspectives and contributions. Reflect on your particular and unique self-expression. Ask others if they understand your point of view. Give them feedback on their contributions and points of view. Ask for feedback on yours. Follow a sharing model—you give something of yourself and you receive something from others. Reflect before you act.

Action Planning

Adapt and apply any ideas from the session to your own team building. Review the basic question asked in the mini-case study: "How can these four individuals build the team the senator wants?" and review the group's answers. Consider the two flip-chart lists of key words, how they differed or were similar. Take action based on careful analysis.

22
········

Needs of Team Members

···

Stop, look, and listen

● PURPOSE

Working in a team involves a different, more personal, kind of communication. The purpose of this session is to define team needs at this company in order to improve relationships and communication.

● SUMMARY

Teamwork is different from working toward performance standards as an individual. The needs of team members are different from the needs of individual workers, especially as they involve communication and other skills of building interpersonal relationships. In this activity, participants are required to use their imaginations as they consider the team practice of writing thank you notes and how these thank you notes suggest the needs of team members who are senders and receivers of the notes. Before the end of the session, participants will turn their attention to team needs analysis practices in this company.

● AGENDA

Step	Time
Discuss examples in the Discussion Starter Handout	15 minutes
Provide examples from the workplace	15 minutes
Describe current and desired practices in this workplace	15 minutes
Wrap up	10 minutes

● INTRODUCTION

1. As participants enter the room, distribute copies of the Discussion Starter Handout and ask them to read it, thinking about the expressed or unexpressed needs of the six team members in the examples. Tell them that these are imaginary employees, and that they'll have to use their imaginations as they look at these examples. Allow 3 to 5 minutes for this.

2. Begin the session by introducing the topic and why it's important:

    "We're here today to talk about the needs of team members and how these differ from the needs of individual workers. Teams are called on to do work together, with a common goal. This kind of work demands finer-tuned communication and relationship building and sustaining skills. Often, however, our hurried lifestyle and work style makes us pay little attention to the kinds of things team members need in order to do the work as teams.

    "The thank you notes of the Discussion Starter Handout involve six individuals on a team. Be sure that you have a copy in front of you as we begin this session. Imagine the situation in which, as an exercise in learning how to work together effectively as a team, the team leader suggests that each member of the team write a thank you note to someone else on the team. These are three of the kinds of thank you notes that were written. The analysis of the thank you notes can provide the team with a statement of needs of the team members who are named in the notes. Imagine the extension of this kind of 'thank you process' to all members of your team or teams in this company. Persons in the Discussion Starter Handout are Carla, Manuel, John, Scott, Neshira, and Noel. A creative exercise like this is an alternative to the typical questionnaire asking team members to specify their needs. In the case here, defining needs requires creative analysis of the issues suggested by each writer."

● AWARENESS

3. Lead a discussion about the three thank you notes that suggest some needs of the six team members involved. Stay with an analysis of the thank you notes handout for about 10 minutes. Don't worry about the "imaginary" people. A careful analysis of these interactions can set the stage later in the session for the same kinds of analytical approaches to team needs at this company. Start the discussion by asking the group to comment on these questions:

- Do you think that Carla might be a good mentor to Manuel in a more formal way? If so, how would you begin to establish a formal mentoring program for these two?

- Could the Manuel/Carla interaction perhaps be a model for a "coaching needs analysis" among other team members too? What topics would you include?

- Could the John/Scott exchange indicate that a team talent bank might be a very useful thing to add to the team's knowledge base? What are the useful categories of workplace talent?

- Do the apparent different job levels and personalities of John and Scott suggest that cross-functioning teams can be very empowering and useful to the company in ways not always imagined when they were organized? Describe situations in which cross-functioning works.

- Noel has a clear need for training in managing his piles of information. If you were in charge, how would you pair him up with Neshira for learning? Would you first check to be sure Neshira has some training or coaching skills and would you provide extra time for her to take on a training task? How would you handle the time issue?

- As a team leader, are you willing to adjust individual productivity targets to encourage team members to handle the extra tasks of defining needs and taking action to meet them? What kinds of flexibility do team leaders need most?

● EXAMPLES

4. Now change the focus of this *Lunch and Learn* session to examples from teams in this company. Focus specifically on ways in which team members' needs as team members are discovered and defined. Ask the group to focus attention on their own team to find examples here of how they discover the needs of their own team members. Challenge them to think of both the informal ways and the intentionally created organizational structures through which team members' needs are made known. Some examples might include games and training activities, periodic surveys, interviews, study of journals, and so on.

5. Ask for a volunteer from the group to record examples on the flip chart. As items are written on the flip chart, seek comments about them from the group. As you lead discussion about workplace examples, keep the focus on the needs of team members.

6. Don't let the comments digress into complaints. However, be prepared for some remarks about teams that don't work very well. Here are some of the things you might hear; if you do, turn them around as a definition of need that can be addressed.

   • "No commitment." Turn it around to "Be sure goals and instructions are clear so that everyone understands exactly what to do. Provide training so that team members gain confidence and are not afraid to commit to helping each other."

   • "No trust." Turn it around to "Pay attention to communication across boundaries so that egos and status don't get in the way. Figure out ways to break down those barriers."

   Let the participants go on identifying examples, but jump in to focus on needs and solutions.

● DEFINITION

7. Referring to any items on the flip charts, ask participants now to come up with an "actionable" statement or list of team members' needs in this company. Ask for a volunteer scribe to start a new flip-chart page. Challenge the group to evaluate the work processes, standards, leadership, communication, and anything else they can think of. Reiterate that this is an exercise in defining the needs of team members here. Suggest any of these possibilities to start.

Tell them that these are hypothetical situations, not necessarily needs of team members here:

- *Recognition.* This company has a culture of individualism and it's hard for people to work in teams where the team gets all the credit. Can we find a way to give employees who've made a unique contribution to the team some individual recognition in addition to recognizing the team?

- *Information sharing.* Within our teams, we have good databases, procedures, computers, and encouragement to share information that has benefit for the entire team. However, we don't have procedures or encouragement to share information among teams. Each team is its own little kingdom. Can we develop a mandate and procedures for sharing among teams?

- *Corporate intelligence.* Teams do work in this company. In fact, teamwork has made substantial contributions to our internal knowledge base. As team members become accustomed to the productivity benefits and good results of working as a team, we seem to have lost sight of corporate goals and status of the company's financial health. Can we develop a structure and procedure for keeping team members up-to-date on corporate intelligence so we can have a better view of where our teamwork fits into the whole picture?

8. After the list of needs has been made, ask the group for ideas about specific programs, projects, approaches, supports, and modifications that could be developed to meet these needs.

● WRAP UP

9. To close the session, refer to the list of needs on the last flip chart (Step 7). Restate the reality that teams are everywhere in today's workplaces, but often team leaders and team members don't pay enough attention to carefully defining the needs of team members. Teamwork is different from working as an individual, and it needs special attention from those committed to its success.

10. Tell participants that time doesn't permit specific action planning in this session, but they should leave this room aware and challenged to define and meet the special needs of team members. The Self-Examination, Reflection, and Action Planning Handout will help them organize their thoughts. Distribute this as they leave the session.

DISCUSSION STARTER HANDOUT FOR
Needs of Team Members

....

Thank You Notes

Team members have been encouraged to write thank you notes to persons anywhere in the company who have been helpful to them. These are some that have been received. Read them to gain some understanding of the needs of team members.

Dear Carla,

You have made such a difference in my life and I wanted to thank you, as we both go forward into the next adventure. You are more than a colleague to me—you are an inspiration and source of the best information!

Sincerely,

Manuel

Dear John,

I never write thank you notes. But I think I could be persuaded. I'm not much of a writer, but just putting pen to paper makes me think of my plain good luck at being on your team. If you ever need somebody to be in charge of refreshments at your board meetings, let me know if I can help. I love to make fancy appetizers.

Sincerely,

Scott

Dear Neshira,

I admire your way of keeping track of things. I need to learn a way to stay organized. I only know how to pile stuff up. Could you explain to me how you organize your files and papers and if your system would work for me?

You're the best!

Noel

SELF-EXAMINATION, REFLECTION, AND ACTION PLANNING HANDOUT FOR
Needs of Team Members

. . . .

Self-Examination

Talk with others on your team about their needs as team members. Be open, build bridges of understanding, graciously give and receive feedback, and demonstrate that you value your own as well as others' ideas and needs. Evaluate the processes in use in your team for assessing needs of team members and say why they are working or why they are not working. Be guided by the words "I think," "I believe," "I understand," and "I value" as you talk and work with colleagues and team members. "I think," "I believe," "I understand," and "I value" are all ways *in* to self-discovery and *out* to better communication and more useful action.

Reflection

Reflect on the balance between individual productivity and performance goals and the productivity and performance goals of your team. Reflect on what individuals on your team particularly need in order to learn, perform, and succeed.

Action Planning

List some action items that you can take in order to accurately, systematically, and creatively assess needs of the members of your team. Look in various places for gaps in performance or communication. Define actions that help you yourself, as well as actions that help others. Get in the habit of asking for help and offering help to others.

-
-
-

23
· · · · · · · ·

Strategies of Teamwork

· ·

But it's different being on a team

● **PURPOSE**

Effective teams have strategies of working together to accomplish their goals in various aspects of work. The purpose of this session is to analyze the positives and the negatives in teamwork in terms of three categories: activities of team members, team learning, and external relationships.

● **SUMMARY**

Defining strategies of teamwork is a necessary first step in planning positive action for the team: teamwork doesn't happen just because you want it to or someone in your company thinks it's a good idea. In this session, participants will focus on three major categories of teamwork—activities of team members, team learning, and external relationships—and consider the strategies that can help team members work together.

● AGENDA

Step	Time
Discuss the symbol in the Discussion Starter Handout	10 minutes
Provide examples from the workplace	15 minutes
Describe current and desired practices in the workplace	25 minutes
Wrap up	5 minutes

● PREPARATION

Make three copies per person of the Definition Handout.

● INTRODUCTION

1. As participants enter the room, distribute copies of the Discussion Starter Handout and ask them to read it.

2. Begin the session by introducing the topic and why it's important:

   "Teamwork doesn't happen just because you want it to or someone in your company thinks it's a good idea. Effective teams have strategies of working together to accomplish their goals in various aspects of work. There are many ways to think about strategies of teamwork, and for this session, we'll focus on three of the major categories of teamwork that require strategic development: activities of team members, team learning, and external relationships.

   "The handout you received contains the yin/yang symbol in association with three major categories of teamwork: activities of team members, team learning, and external relationships. Seeing the three categories each as a yin/yang symbol can be a way into understanding the complexities of strategies of teamwork. Any session on strategy begins with analysis."

3. As participants are referring to the handout, write these words on the flip chart:

   • Activities

   • Learning

   • External relationships

   Tell participants that the yin/yang symbol represents light and shadow, change and stasis, order and chaos, positives and negatives, becoming and being, opportunity and crisis—representations of the dynamic opposites of life. Challenge them to use the symbol as a way to begin to think about strategies and their positive and negative sides.

4. Tell participants that they'll first talk about how team activities differ from individual activities, and suggest that they think in terms of a "yin/yang" approach; that is, ask them to think about the bad things and the good things about team activities. Lead a discussion about the "crisis/opportunity," "negative/positive," and "darkness/light" characteristics of the yin/yang symbol. Use these kinds of questions to help guide discussion:

   • If you were organizing a workplace team, what kinds of activities would you plan?

   • From a team perspective, what are the positives and negatives of these activities?

   • How do team activities differ from activities planned for individual workers?

   • What kinds of team activities could easily turn into crises?

   • What kinds of work activities lend themselves to a team approach?

   • How can the work activities of teams be prevented from becoming crises and instead become opportunities? Instead of darkness, shed light?

5. After about 10 minutes of discussion using the yin/yang symbol in this analysis exercise, move into the other two major categories, team learning and external relationships. These two categories require a similar kind of analysis.

---

6. Tell participants now to think about team learning and about how learning in teams is different from an individual worker's going to a training seminar. As they begin to analyze the pluses and minuses of team learning, lead them in a listing of "learning problems" and "learning solutions" and have them think in terms of the yin/yang symbol again. Ask for a volunteer scribe to make the lists on a flip chart. Ask the general question: "Is this a problem or a solution?" Here are some questions for facilitating discussion of team learning:

   • What percentage of team learning happens on the job, as opposed to in a classroom?

   • Is this a positive or a negative? A problem or a solution? Why? (Add the response to the flip chart in the appropriate list.)

   • Are team members more open to new ideas when they are learning than are individual learners? Why? (Add the response to the flip chart in the appropriate list.)

   • Are there fewer obstacles to learning in a team than as an individual? What are these obstacles? (Add the response to the flip chart in the appropriate list.)

   • Do team members accept and exhibit more responsibility as both teachers and learners than do individuals at work? (Add the response to the flip chart in the appropriate list.)

   • Do team members have the skills they need to be both teacher and learner? (Add the response to the flip chart in the appropriate list.)

   • How do you know whether or not learning has occurred in a team? (Add the response to the flip chart in the appropriate list.)

   Continue the discussion by asking whether anyone has any other comments about team learning, and record their comments on the flip chart in the appropriate lists.

7. Now move on to an analysis of a team's external relationships. Tell participants to think of these relationships from a strategy point of view. Suggest that they think about the concepts of connection, collaboration, integration, roles, communication, feedback, and corrective action. Ask for a volunteer scribe to record responses on the flip chart, as in Step 6. Title the lists "darkness" and "light." Use these kinds of questions to start the discussion about examples in

the category of external relationships; decide as a group on which list the responses belong:

- Are the obstacles to presenting a united front to important external "others" (suppliers, customers, the press, community organizations) more severe or less severe in teamwork than in individual work?

- Are e-mail and other online communication structures a help or a hindrance to teams in external communications? Why?

- Is it harder or easier to "fix" a broken external relationship if you are organized as a team?

Ask the group for any other ideas they have about the yin and yang of a team's external relationships. Record any additional comments on the "darkness and light" flip chart.

● DEFINITION

8. Distribute three copies of the Definition Handout to each participant.

9. Explain to participants that they will now focus on specific characteristics and strategies of teamwork in their own teams or on other teams in this company with which they are familiar. Remind the group that this is a DEFINITION exercise, that is, participants will state *what they do* or describe *what is*—the negative activities of team members and the positive activities of team members in today's current teams. These are the instructions to participants for completing the exercise:

- Choose one category per handout sheet. Put a checkmark next to the category you choose to analyze: Activities of Team Members, Team Learning, or External Relationships.

- Name the yin/yang dichotomy you want to use in this analysis (for example, crisis/opportunity, darkness/light, minuses/pluses, and so on) and write it on the line.

- Be specific in your analysis of your own team behavior and experiences. List characteristics in both sides of the yin/yang symbol. Write in the margins corresponding to each side of the symbol. Complete at least one of these handout sheets; use all three of them if you have time. Focus this exercise on defining the current situation.

10. After about 10 minutes, ask for volunteers to read their handouts to the group. Ask for comments from other participants. Tell the group to respect different learning styles and levels of emotional involvement.

11. Ask by show of hands how many in the group analyzed the first category, Activities of Team Members? The second category, Team Learning? And the third category, External Relationships? Choose a category in which the most participation was indicated, and try now to focus on defining a strategy based on the group's analyses. Ask for a volunteer to use his or her analysis to suggest a statement of strategy. For example, if a negative such as "too informal, needs more structure" were listed in the Team Learning category, a strategy might be:

To meet with an instructional designer to help us figure out the best ways to develop the training we need.

Record responses on a flip chart. Continue to ask volunteers to make statements of strategies of teamwork until at least one strategy is completed in each of the three categories. Encourage reaction from the group and discussion about the volunteers' statements.

● WRAP UP

12. Close the session by reiterating the importance and the uniqueness of strategies of teamwork. Urge participants to approach their work as teams with a fresh sense of analysis and definition of working together as teams.

13. Distribute a copy of the Self-Examination, Reflection, and Action Planning Handout to each participant and explain that participants can use this worksheet to help organize their thoughts.

DISCUSSION STARTER HANDOUT FOR
Strategies of Teamwork

Yin/Yang Symbol

Activities of Team Members

Team Learning

External Relationships

HANDOUT 23.2

DEFINITION HANDOUT FOR
Strategies of Teamwork

· ·

_____ Activities of team members

_____ Team learning

_____ External relationships

(name of the dichotomy)

Negatives

Positives

HANDOUT 23.3

SELF-EXAMINATION, REFLECTION, AND ACTION PLANNING HANDOUT FOR
Strategies of Teamwork

• •

Self-Examination and Reflection

Think about your personal strengths and weaknesses and what they contribute to or detract from the work of the team as a team. Consider such things as tolerance for ambiguity, mental flexibility, openness to new ideas and new people, intellectual curiosity and risk taking, emotional strength, competency at both systematic thinking and abstract thinking, and so on. Make a list of these and other strengths and weaknesses and give yourself a plus or a minus on each of these items.

- •

- •

- •

- •

           •

           •

           •

           •

Action Planning

Resolve to take some kind of action in an area where you can make a positive difference in the work of your team. Focus on corrections in the kinds of things you do or the ways in which you do them, the ways in which you inhibit or promote team learning, and what you personally can do to improve relationships with employees, departments, customers, or community leaders external to your team. Make this resolution in the form of journal entries or plans, whatever style of documentation motivates you into action based on analysis. Share your ideas with other members of your team or with others in the *Lunch and Learn* session who can support your actions.

24
. . . .

Team Resources

. . . .

Pay attention, clarify, be assertive

● PURPOSE

Teams need many kinds of resources and companies need to provide many kinds of support to them in order to promote effective teamwork. The purpose of this session is to identify resources needed by teams in this company and to identify processes required to acquire them.

● SUMMARY

It is helpful to think about resources in a deliberate way, so that careful planning can follow in order to get them. In this activity, participants will individually define the resources they need, after which they will share their definitions with the group as a whole. The activity will use "recipe cards" that identify both the ingredients and the process required to obtain a particular team resource.

● AGENDA

Step	Time
Discuss the Discussion Starter Handout	5 minutes
Provide examples from the workplace	20 minutes
Define current and desired practices in the workplace	20 minutes
Wrap up	10 minutes

● INTRODUCTION

1. As participants enter the room distribute copies of the Discussion Starter Handout and ask them to study it.

2. Begin the session by introducing the topic and why it's important:

   "We're here today to talk about team resources. We know that there are many different kinds of resources that teams need in order to do effective teamwork, including networked technology; human relations interventions such as mentoring and coaching; training that's unique to teamwork; stretch job assignments; recognition; rewards; communication; social events; equality of opportunity; feedback; appropriate accountability standards; developmental learning opportunities; access to personnel; access to information; and so on.

   "The handout you received has the outline of a recipe card drawn on it, with a space in the tab to specify 'the resource' and spaces for the 'ingredients' and the 'process' required to make it happen. Later in the session, you'll develop some of your own resource recipes and share them with the group here."

● AWARENESS

3. Begin the session with a discussion about the kinds of resources that teams need. Ask the group for their ideas. Ask them which of the resources you just mentioned are important to them. Write these important ones on a flip chart;

ask whether there are any other kinds of needed team resources that should be added to the list. Keep the discussion going until participants seem satisfied that you've listed the most important resources.

Ask for a show of hands indicating how many participants agree with each item on the flip chart. If participants want to talk or "let off steam," keep the discussion going by challenging them with the simple questions: "Why is this important to you?" or "Why is this important to your team?"

● EXAMPLES

4. Distribute one Recipe Cards Handout to each person. Refer the group back to the Discussion Starter Handout for an example of the task ahead. The goal of the exercise is for each participant to create four recipes for needed team resources at this company. Each card will contain one identified resource. When the group's recipe cards have all been created, you will have a definition of team resources. Allow about 20 minutes for this activity.

5. These are the instructions for completing the exercise, following the example on the Discussion Starter Handout:

   • Write the name of the needed team resource on the tab at the top of the recipe card; for example, PERFORMANCE MEASURES.

   • Then list the ingredients you believe the team needs in order to demonstrate that the topic of the recipe card is being addressed: for example, budget numbers, accounting, team targets, quality standards.

   • Now describe the processes by which the ingredients will be acted on. Be as creative as you are moved to be in this task; for example, use cooking terminology if you're feeling especially innovative—such as "stir in . . . ," "mix thoroughly . . . ," "chill . . . ," "blend . . . ," "wait . . . ," "shape into . . . ," and so on. Or simply specify typical (or atypical) business processes to act on the ingredients you've listed.

   • For example, in the PERFORMANCE MEASURES "recipe," you might suggest processes like these: "adhere religiously to . . . ," "provide some wiggle room in . . . ," "verify accuracy with each team member . . . ," "share critical data regarding . . . ," "develop monitoring and evaluation systems regarding . . . ," "choose an accountability buddy for feedback," and so on. Begin the "Process" list with verbs—action words.

- Here are some other suggestions for "recipes":

    BUSINESS PLANS

    TRAINING SEMINARS

    COACHING TIME ON THE JOB

    TALENT DATA BANK

    JOB ROTATION

    TECHNOLOGY UPDATE

    Choose any of these that might be important for your teams at this company, refer to the flip-chart lists, or state your own category of resource need.

- Complete the four recipe cards, or as many of them as you can.

● DEFINITION

6. This recipe card exercise can help to define the resources required by teams at this company. Ask participants now to share their best cards with the group. Ask for volunteers to read one or more of their "recipes" to the group. Aim to have participants express a variety of resource needs.

7. Ask group participants whose "recipes" got laughs or loud comments from others in the group to write their best recipe on a flip-chart page, one per page. Tear off each recipe (get at least four from the group to post) from the flip chart and post it on the wall.

    Suggest that careful definition involves detailed analysis, action processes, and the special purposes of teams.

● WRAP UP

8. End the session with a final exercise in analysis and extracting a list of team resource needs identified in the recipe cards. Write the list on the flip chart, or ask for a volunteer to do this. Involve as many participants as possible—go for quantity of response. It's okay to be directive to ask for more responses: for example, say "How about you?" "So what did you think?" or "Can you think of one related to that?" Encourage group examination of ideas.

9. Distribute a copy of the Self-Examination, Reflection, and Action Planning Handout to each participant and explain that they can use this worksheet as they define resource needs for their teams. Note that this is two pages.

DISCUSSION STARTER HANDOUT FOR
Team Resources

. . . .

Recipe Cards

This Discussion Starter Handout is an activity in the form of a learning game, an exercise in identifying and beginning the development of resources that your teams at this company need.

Sample Recipe Card

networked computers

Ingredients:

- *6 new computers, printers, scanners*

- *new wiring*

- *a place in I.T.'s budget*

- *installers*

Process:

- *identify hardware we want in the catalog*

- *be sure space is adequate in each office*

- *find out I.T.'s budget cycle*

- *meet with I.T. decision-makers*

Source: Adapted from "Recipe for Success," in *More Team Games for Trainers* (pp. 119–121) by C. Nilson. New York: McGraw-Hill, 1998. Copyright © The McGraw-Hill Companies, Inc. Used with permission.

RECIPE CARDS HANDOUT FOR
Team Resources

Ingredients:

Process:

Ingredients:

Process:

Ingredients:

Process:

Ingredients:

Process:

SELF-EXAMINATION, REFLECTION, AND ACTION PLANNING HANDOUT FOR
Team Resources

. . . .

Self-Examination

Think about how you defined your own resource needs as a team member. List them and prioritize them, greatest need to least need.

-
-
-
-
-

Reflection

Then reflect on the resource needs of other participants in the *Lunch and Learn* session. Modify your own needs, if necessary, according to the needs of others as they relate to your needs.

Action Planning

Choose five team resource needs that you believe especially apply to the needs of your team. Prioritize them in the sequence in which you, personally, will take action to enhance your team's resources. Identify the actions you will take.

1.

2.

3.

4.

5.

25
· · · · · · · · ·

Team Vision

· ·

Yes, but how do we get there?

● PURPOSE

The purpose of this session is to examine several vision statements and declarations of values, including those from the Olympic Games, in order to develop a realistic vision for teams in this company.

● SUMMARY

Team vision is an important part of teamwork and we need to take care that vision is defined in a way that enlightens and encourages individuals on the team to work for the team. Too often, vision statements are good words only, with no possibility of workers ever reaching the vision. In this activity, participants will first discuss the Olympic vision from the Athens Games and then analyze examples of vision statements in order to define a useful vision for their teams.

● AGENDA

Step	Time
Discuss the example in the Discussion Starter Handout	15 minutes
Discuss workplace examples	15 minutes
Describe current and desired practices in the workplace	15 minutes
Wrap up	10 minutes

● INTRODUCTION

1. As participants enter the room, distribute copies of the Discussion Starter Handout and ask them to study it.

2. Begin the session by introducing the topic and why it's important:

   "Team vision is an important part of teamwork and we need to take care that vision is defined in a way that enlightens and encourages individuals on the team to work for the team. Too often, vision statements are good words only, with no possibility of workers ever reaching the vision.

   "'Heritage, Human Scale, and Participation'—these are the stated values of the Olympic Games held in Athens, Greece, in 2004. These values were the compass that guided this expression of vision and celebration for humankind. The flame ignited by the sun in March 2004 eventually lit the torch of a Greek javelin champion, who then began the relay of the flame and torch for the first time in Olympic history to all six continents. The symbol of the Olympic Torch is a powerful one.

   "In a business or an organization, the vision creators are encouraged to think direction and purpose, values and customer service. Logic, analysis, control, and efficiency are not the language of vision. Understanding vision is sometimes made easier by thinking of vision as a compass and management as a roadmap. In this activity, we'll first discuss the Olympic vision and then analyze examples of vision statements in order to define a useful vision for your own teams."

● AWARENESS

3. Continue by saying the following:

   "Consider the differences between these two statements of vision:

   - We will be a world class army.

   - This nation should commit itself to the objective of landing a man on the moon and bringing him back safely to earth within this decade.

   "The first statement is 'all sizzle and no steak'; the desire to become world class is simply too vague. It would be too easy to smile at this vision statement and dismiss it. Civilian employees and soldiers would be hard pressed to understand exactly what they were aiming for in the conduct of their jobs. The second statement is the vision of President John F. Kennedy prior to the start of the Apollo moon launch program. It is visionary, lofty, value-laden, emotionally appealing, carries with it strong symbolism, and is suggestive of measurements along the process of working within that vision."

4. Refer back now to the Discussion Starter Handout, specifically to the symbolism of the torch. Ask participants these questions:

   - Consider the torch: What about the materials used to create the torch, the lighting of the torch, or the carrying of the torch inspires you?

   - Consider the 2004 Olympic values: How do you relate to "heritage, human scale, and participation"? Would you add any other values to these three, based on your understanding of or involvement with the Olympics? What would these be?

5. Lead a discussion about Olympic symbols and values.

● EXAMPLES

6. Direct participants' attention now to examples from their own experience with teams. Write the words "What," Who," How," and "When" on a flip chart so that they are headings for four columns, which the group will fill in with their

ideas about these aspects of vision. Use the "man on the moon and back" vision as an example:

What	Who	How	When
man on the moon and back	the nation	safely	within the decade

Ask the group for samples from their own experience to add to the flip chart's four headings. Tell them that their "visions" can come from community groups, from family, from educational institutions, from medical establishments, or from their work experience. Fill in the group's words under the appropriate what, who, how, and when columns and lead a discussion around their ideas.

● **DEFINITION**

7. Move on to the specifics of this company, according to the What, Who, How, and When model. Focus on using this simple four-part guideline as a way to make sure their values "have legs." Ask participants to turn their attention to defining a vision for their teams or for this company. Encourage the group to deal with a comprehensive statement, considering the What, the Who, the How, and the When that should give a vision statement some shape. Ask for a volunteer to record ideas from the group on the flip chart as you facilitate the discussion.

8. Ask for a show of hands about how many in the room can state this company's or their team's vision or mission statement. Ask a volunteer to say it now and see how it fits within the ideas of this *Lunch and Learn* session. Ask participants to share their positive and negative comments with each other. The following questions can help guide the discussion:

   • Does it fit in the categories on the flip chart?

   • Does your team have multiple visions?

   • Would the vision for the team be helped if it fit within the columns on the flip chart?

- Can you revise or modify current terminology in use to add something important to it (for example, emotional appeal, personal challenge, clear benefit for the persons involved, employees, stakeholders or community)? Remember to think "compass" and not "roadmap" at this stage of thinking. Direction is what's important now; details come later as management takes over.

- Can you think in terms of value-laden actions by leaders and by ordinary workers—words like develop, focus, share, and model, for example? Can you think of other values that can shape a definition of team vision here—descriptive words such as enthusiastic, adventuresome, committed?

Encourage diverse points of view, keeping the discussion centered on values. Refer to several of the participants' contributions as you conclude the session.

● WRAP UP

9. To close the session, reiterate the importance of a credible yet challenging team vision.

10. Tell participants that the handout they are about to receive can serve as a worksheet for them as they refine their team's vision, or as they create a new team vision. Challenge participants to remember the symbolism and the values in the Olympic Games, and to remember the simple four-category job aid to help them think more clearly.

11. Distribute a copy of the Self-Examination, Reflection, and Action Planning Handout to each participant as they leave the session. Note that it is two pages.

HANDOUT 25.1
DISCUSSION STARTER HANDOUT FOR
Team Vision

The Olympic Flame and Torch

The flame of the Athens 2004 Summer Olympic Games was lit in Olympia, Greece, on March 25, 2004. The silver-colored magnesium and olive wood torch in the shape of an elongated olive leaf is said to embody the leaf's harmonious shape and upward dynamic.

SELF-EXAMINATION, REFLECTION, AND ACTION PLANNING HANDOUT FOR

Team Vision

• •

Self-Examination

Take a few minutes to examine your own ways of contributing to working toward your team's vision.

Consider your own shortcomings regarding response to vision, share these with others on your team, and ask for help or feedback. Say please and thank you in a spirit of withholding judgment and of reaffirming self-examination. Remember what was said in the *Lunch and Learn* session. Work to define an actionable vision that goes beyond beautiful words.

Reflection

One of the strategies needed for embracing a team vision is that of sharing understanding more quickly in order to tap into the multiple perspectives that are always apparent in a group of individuals. It's hard work to listen without prejudice. Another is to demonstrate ways in which to work through conflicts and remove barriers to collaboration. It's easier to fake it, stay out of other people's way, and pretend to be in harmony with all around you. Team visions are not realized by that kind of withdrawal from purpose and denial of problems. Teams at work will exhibit energies that defeat lofty visions—aggression, ego trips, sulking, silence, and resignation are just some of these.

Action Planning

Define at least two ways in which you personally can contribute to team vision. This can be by helping to revise or enhance the vision or mission statements and other written goals and value-focused materials, or it can be by developing an individual performance excellence vision for yourself that addresses the already-stated team vision. As you begin this planning, think of the Olympic Torch relay on six continents, the Olympic values of "heritage, human scale, and participation," the lighting of the fire by the sun, and the examples mentioned in this session. Share your thoughts and plans with others on your team; begin collaboration now, building into it vision that reflects your unique personalities and corporate perspectives. Set a date for discussion and stick to it.

-

-

-

-

About the Author

....

Carolyn Nilson, Ed.D., is a recognized expert in all aspects of training. Corporate training positions have included work as a Member of Technical Staff at AT&T Bell Laboratories, where she was part of the Advanced Programs, Standards, and Inspections Group of the Systems Training Center. She implemented and promoted quality standards in training design, delivery, and evaluation throughout AT&T. In addition, she taught the Bell Labs' train-the-trainer course. Dr. Nilson also served as manager of simulation training at Combustion Engineering (CE) for Asea Brown Boveri, where she managed the training operation, including the creation of high-level computer-based simulation training for international clients in Norway, Germany, Canada, Venezuela, Saudi Arabia, and China. At CE, she was on a corporation-wide training design team using expert system technologies to create an electronic performance support system (EPSS) in learner evaluation. Dr. Nilson held the executive position of director of training for a management consulting firm with a broad-based Fortune 500 clientele in the New York City area, where she was responsible for budgets and consultant staff supervision as well as for training analysis, design, development, implementation, and evaluation on client projects. Corporations she has served include AT&T, Chemical Bank, Chevron, Nabisco, Martin-Marietta, Dun & Bradstreet, National Westminster Bank, and others. She has been an adviser to the American Management Association/AMACOM Books, Hungry Minds, Brandon Hall, and The MASIE Center and a faculty member for Padgett-Thompson seminars throughout the U.S., The Ziff Institute, The Center for the Study of Work Teams in Dallas, Texas, and The Egypt-U.S. Presidents' (Mubarek-Clinton) Council's Management Development Initiative in Cairo, Egypt, through Pal-Tech, Inc., Arlington, Virginia.

She has also been a consultant to government organizations in the areas of training design, delivery, evaluation, and management. These organizations include The World Bank, U.S. Department of Labor, U.S. Department of Education, The National Institute of Education, The U.S. Armed Services Training Institute, and the U.S. Agency for International Development (USAID). She has been a speaker at conferences of ASTD, ISPI, and the American Management Association (AMA). Her work has been featured in *TRAINING Magazine, Training & Development (T + D), HR Magazine, Successful Meetings, Entrepreneur, Fortune,* and *The Pfeiffer Annual.* She is the author of numerous training papers, speeches, articles, manuals, and books; her writings are selling worldwide to a diverse customer base. Four of her books appeared in Amazon.com's list of "50 Best-Selling Training Books." She is a Schwartz Business Books 1995 "Celebrity Author" (Milwaukee, WI) and was on the 1996 "This Year's Best Sellers" of Newbridge Book Clubs (Delran, NJ). Her books have also been chosen by Macmillan's Executive Program Book Club, The Training Professionals Book Club, and the *Business Week* Book Club.

Carolyn Nilson received her doctorate from Rutgers University with a specialty in measurement and evaluation in technical education. She earned an MS degree, cum laude, in educational administration/business administration and a BA degree in history. Books by Carolyn Nilson include:

2004	*The Performance Consulting Textbook,* (Chinese ed.), Science and Culture, Hong Kong
2004	*AMA Trainers' Activity Book,* AMACOM
2003	*How to Manage Training* (3rd ed.), with CD-ROM, AMACOM
2002	*How to Start a Training Program,* ASTD
1999	*Como Formar a su personal,* Ediciones Juan Granica, Buenos Aires
1999	*The Performance Consulting Toolbook,* McGraw-Hill
1998	*How to Manage Training* (2nd ed.), AMACOM
1998	*More Team Games for Trainers,* McGraw-Hill
1998	*Complete Games Trainers Play, Vol. II* (co-author), McGraw-Hill
1996–2002	*Training & Development Yearbook,* Prentice Hall
1995	*Games That Drive Change,* McGraw-Hill
1994	*Training for Non-Trainers* (Spanish Edition), Ediciones Juan Granica, Buenos Aires
1993	*Team Games for Trainers,* McGraw-Hill
1991	*Training for Non-Trainers, A Do-It-Yourself Guide for Managers,* AMACOM
1989	*Training Program Workbook and Kit,* Prentice Hall